PRAISE FOR *GET THE FAT OUT*

"Victoria Moran has artfully compiled 501 of the best tips ever for reducing the fat in all of your favorite dishes. Plus, she interprets the rules for eating right in a compassionate and easy-to-understand manner. I heartily recommend this book to every health-conscious cook."
—Kathryn Arnold, Food Editor,
Delicious! magazine

"This is more than just a recipe book. It gives practical guidelines to prepare and purchase the foods *you like best* while still eating a healthy diet."
—Carlos A. Dujovne, M.D., Professor of Medicine and Director, Lipid and Arteriosclerosis Prevention Clinic, University of Kansas, School of Medicine and Leslie Votaw, M.S., R.D.

"*Get the Fat Out* is full of valuable and innovative ideas—a great beginning to a healthy way of eating. Everyone should own it."
—Lindsay Wagner, actress, and Ariane Spade, coauthors of *High Road to Health*

"A marvelously creative addition toward techniques of optimal nutrition."
—Caldwell B. Esselstyn, Jr., M.D., Director and Program Chairman, 1st National Conference on the Elimination of Coronary Artery Disease

"As people turn to low-fat diets, they need help. This book goes a long way in providing that."
— Julian Whitaker, M.D., author of *Reversing Heart Disease*, *Reversing Diabetes*, and *Reversing Health Risks*

"When Victoria turns her attention to an issue, she covers *every* detail. This is a book for every cook!"
— Marilyn Diamond, author of *The American Vegetarian Cookbook from the Fit for Life Kitchen*

"*Get the Fat Out: 501 Simple Ways to Cut the Fat in Any Diet* is a good book for anyone who wants to lower his or her dietary fat. It not only explains the role of fat in our diets, but also gives some very practical steps for addressing the issue creatively and positively—in one's kitchen where the issue will finally be resolved."
— Ronald Pickarski, author of *Friendly Foods* and President and Certified Executive Chef for Eco-Cuisine, Inc.

"In this well-researched, practical, and readable book, Victoria Moran combines her usual impressive knowledge with her love of delicious natural food to make *Get the Fat Out* a valuable tool for the transition toward healthy eating in the twenty-first century."
— Michael Klaper, M.D., Director Institute of Nutrition Education and Research

GET THE
FAT OUT

501 Simple Ways to Cut
the Fat in Any Diet

Victoria Moran

CROWN TRADE PAPERBACKS, NEW YORK

Published by Crown Publishers, Inc., 201 East 50th Street, New York,
New York 10022. Member of the Crown Publishing Group.
Random House, Inc. New York, Toronto, London, Sydney, Auckland
CROWN TRADE PAPERBACKS and colophon are trademarks of
Crown Publishers, Inc.
Manufactured in U.S.A.

Design by M. Kristen Bearse

Library of Congress Cataloging-in-Publication Data
Moran, Victoria
Get the fat out: 501 simple ways to cut the fat in any diet /
Victoria Moran.—1st ed.
Includes bibliographical references.
1. Low-fat diet. I. Title.
RM237.7.M677 1994
613.2'8—dc20
93-39792
CIP

ISBN 0-517-88184-5
10 9 8 7 6 5 4 3 2 1
First Edition

To my mother,
Gladys Marshall

A great cook,
the old way and the new

ACKNOWLEDGMENTS

I wish to thank my literary agent, Patti Breitman, for inspiring me about this topic, encouraging me to write *Get the Fat Out*, and working with me every chapter of the way; my editor at Crown-Harmony Books, Peter Guzzardi; his assistant, Sarah Hamlin; and everyone else there for their good work; and Suzanne Havala, M.S., R.D., and Neal Barnard, M.D., for their foreword and introduction to this book. And I wish to acknowledge Stan Rosenfeld and Pete Shifflett for their tireless computer wisdom, and Carol Shifflett and George Demmer for their editorial assistance.

Thanks are also due all the people who provided me with suggestions for these pages. Almost everyone I know came up with something to help in putting together *Get the Fat Out*. Among the health professionals, chefs, food writers, and just good cooks who were particularly generous in sharing ideas and information with me are Mildred Aissen; Nathaniel Altman; Kathryn Arnold; Nava Atlas; Charles Attwood, M.D.; Freya Dinshah; George Eisman, M.S., R.D.; Wendy Fertschneider, R.D.; Chef Michael Forsberg; Elaine French; Michael Klaper, M.D.; Kate Lawrence; Margaret Malone; my mother, Gladys Marshall; Virginia Messina, M.P.H., R.D.; Chef Ron Pickarski; Sonnet Pierce; Jennifer Raymond; and Leslie Votaw, M.S., R.D.

I would also like to thank all the other culinary artists who have allowed their recipes to be reprinted. In addition to those already mentioned, authors such as Marilyn Diamond, Rosalie Hurd, Mary McDougall, Lindsay Wagner and Ariane Spade, and Debra Wasserman have been most instrumental in helping me become a low-fat cook with enough confidence to invite over even the most discriminating diners. No one has gone home hungry yet.

In addition, I want to express my appreciation to all the physicians, dietitians, and researchers who have done the work to show that lowering the fat in our diet can indeed result in a higher level of health and vitality.

On a personal note, I wish to thank the other people who made it possible for me to complete this project: Douglas Graham, D.C.; Suzanne Hatlestad; Lis Jensen; Guru Parwaz Khalsa; Dickey Paldon; Mary and Terry Rouse; Dolores Sehorn; Susan Timmerman; and Carol Wiesner for help in dozens of practical ways; my daughter Rachael Moran for her patience and her bread stick recipe; and Robert Morris for reminding me of the larger world beyond my word processor screen. I also owe a special debt of gratitude to the women of the Wednesday evening success group for opening my eyes to limitless possibilities.

CONTENTS

Using This Book

Foreword by Suzanne Havala, M.S., R.D.

Introduction by Neal D. Barnard, M.D.

Preface—The Facts of Fat

CHAPTER 1 Get the Fat Out of Your Kitchen ▪ *20*

CHAPTER 2 Get the Fat Out of Bread and Breakfast ▪ *35*

CHAPTER 3 Get the Fat Out of Salads, Dressings, and Dips ▪ *51*

CHAPTER 4 Get the Fat Out of Soups and Sauces ▪ *67*

CHAPTER 5 Get the Fat Out of Entrees and Side Dishes ▪ *84*

CHAPTER 6 Get the Fat Out of Sandwiches, Snacks, and Appetizers ▪ *107*

CHAPTER 7 Get the Fat Out of Baking, Desserts, and Treats ▪ *119*

CHAPTER 8 Get the Fat Out When You Eat Out ▪ *141*

CHAPTER 9 Get the Fat Off Your Body and Out of Your Life ▪ *154*

Afterword

Appendix: A Week of Sample Menus

Bibliography

Permissions

Index

About the Author

USING THIS BOOK

To paraphrase Abraham Lincoln, a person's only reasonable hope is to please all of the people some of the time and some of the people all of the time. The tips in this book are aimed at pleasing as many people as much of the time as possible and helping you to better health and more enjoyable dining in the process. These tips will reduce the fat content of your diet in a manner that is easy, effective, delicious, and in some cases downright elegant.

Although using these suggestions will lower the fat content of any diet, one based on whole grains, vegetables, fruits, and legumes is cholesterol free and by definition low in fat. Voluminous research compiled over the past thirty years strongly suggests that a vegetarian or near-vegetarian way of eating is ideal. This is true not only because such a diet is low in fat but also because of its high fiber and complex carbohydrate content, and its abundance of fruits and vegetables that contain substances which actually protect against cancer and other degenerative diseases. This dietary style is also adequate but not excessive in protein, a nutrient that, in surplus, is dangerous, not unlike immoderate amounts of fat.

Therefore, when a tip in this book involves the use of meat or egg products, I have used the notation *inter.* to indicate an intermediate or transitional tip. Choosing those animal products that are lower in fat than others and preparing them without added fats or oils is an important step in the right direction, but I wouldn't be honest if I were to tell you that I believe that step will take you far enough.

My own introduction to low-fat living was as a teenager in 1969 when I learned some of the principles of "the Prudent Diet" developed by Dr. Norman Jolliffe as a result of his pioneering study on coronary heart disease begun in the 1950s. My interest at that time was in losing weight, and I spent a year and a half adapting some of Dr. Jolliffe's advice to my situation. I limited my beef intake to three times a week, increased my fish consumption considerably, ate lots of fresh vegetables, and used no visible fats or oils in or on anything. I did lose weight, but it didn't last. I found the diet too cumbersome—weighing my four-ounce portions of animal protein, and tiring of all the seafood, as if my life stretched before me as an endless Lent: fish, fish, fish.

My continued search for a better way of eating eventually led me to the discovery that eating the foods that grow out of the ground—vegetables, fruits, grains, beans—would enable me to eat without dieting, not weigh or measure anything, and never worry about cholesterol, fat in my arteries, or fat on my thighs. And these foods offer so much variety and color and gustatory pleasure that they're never old hat.

I love the way I eat, but I live in my skin and you live in yours. My job in writing this book is to give you both the best I know and everything else I know on the subject of low-fat eating. The fact is, it was in following Dr. Jolliffe's diet—with meat and fish and four eggs a week, foods I don't eat at all now—that I first learned to prepare tasty meals without using oils or butter. It was a viable start. What's important for you today is to start, or continue, your own adventure in cutting the fat from your diet and adding vitality to your life.

In addition to the basic tips and those marked intermediate, you'll find some with the notation *mod.* for moderate. They are the ones that contain items not particularly low in fat but which offer a superior alternative to the usual choice. When the diet as a whole contains very little fat, most people can enjoy such foods in moderation.

Regular tofu, for example, gets 48 percent of its calories from fat, but it can replace items much higher in fat such as mayonnaise and regular cream cheese—90 percent fat each. And when tofu is part of a meal containing hearty servings of grains and vegetables, the total fat content of the meal is not out of line. In addition, tofu contains no cholesterol.

Because this is a book about lowering fat, I've used the *mod.* indication only as it refers to fat. Moderation is, of course, often the sensible way to proceed. Any time you use concentrated sweeteners (such as sugar, honey, maple syrup), table salt or soy sauce, wine in cooking or brandy in a dessert, it only makes sense to use these judiciously, if at all, depending upon your own physiological and psychological makeup. And because excess protein, like excess fat, can be too much of a good thing, high-protein foods such as nonfat dairy products should also not be used indiscriminately.

The *bonus tips* are not included in the 501 count because they are not specifically about cutting fat. They may, however, add to your culinary IQ, make things easier in the kitchen, or help you toward a healthier, more interesting way of eating.

Most of the ideas in this book can be instantly incorporated into the way you cook and eat right now. When additional detail is required, a recipe is given instead of simply a tip. When I refer to a recipe as "oil free" or "fat free," I mean that no extracted oils or added fats are used. It does not necessarily mean that there is no fat whatsoever in the dish. Almost everything we eat contains some fat: that's how we can get the two essential fatty acids we need without slathering on oily extras.

The majority of the foods used in the tips and recipes are

familiar ones that can be found in any supermarket. When an item is more readily available in a natural foods store or ethnic market, that will be noted. Although you can eat a health-giving, low-fat diet without ever stepping inside a health food store, I encourage you to explore the best natural foods grocery in your area if you haven't already. The products there—from organically grown produce to specialty grains and flours to an array of fat-reduced and fat-free convenience foods—can add markedly to the variety and appeal of low-fat meals.

Many other books are referred to in *Get the Fat Out*, both as sources of recipes and as references for related subjects, such as exercise and nutrition. These are listed in the text by title and author. For full publication data, please refer to the Bibliography. Some product brand names are mentioned here as well. This does not mean that that particular item is the only one available or even necessarily the best, simply that it's the best of its type that I've found.

Do not expect to implement all 501 recommendations. Choose those that sound good to you and that fit the way you live. If you are already a vegetarian, you will gloss over the intermediate tips and any others that don't apply. If you wish to follow a diet free of all extracted oils, the instructions on ways to use smaller amounts of these will not be for you. If your doctor wants you to limit your sodium intake, you will need to skip or modify those hints calling for soy sauce, miso, or other high-sodium ingredients. (Interestingly enough, meat and dairy products provide not only the bulk of saturated fat in the American diet, but most of its sodium as well.)

Even after excluding some of the 501 suggestions to meet your personal needs, hundreds of appropriate ones will remain. If you consistently use even one tenth of those listed, you're sure to cut the fat in your diet and your life in a noticeable way. Let these hints be your springboard to better health and delicious, light cuisine. As you read them and try them out, they'll spark your creativity and you'll find yourself coming up with fat-trimming ideas of your own. Enjoy yourself as you start today to *begin your fat-free adventure!*

FOREWORD

■ BY SUZANNE HAVALA, M.S., R.D. ■

This book is going to drive you crazy. Before you get through the first chapter, you'll be turning down page corners for future reference or flagging passages with Post-Its. You may decide to work through the book section by section, picking and choosing the tips you'd like to try, a few at a time. Suffice it to say, this book is lots of fun!

But most of all this book will *motivate* you to change the way you eat. And you'll see just how easy and enjoyable that can be to do. In *Get the Fat Out*, Victoria Moran shares suggestions for reducing the fat in your diet. Some of the tips are clever, some are simple, and many will make you wonder, "Why didn't somebody tell me this a long time ago?" All of them will be most helpful in assisting you in your transition to a healthier lifestyle.

The biggest surprise awaiting you, though, may be this: when you get the fat out, a whole new world will open up. You'll discover a way of eating that is *so* varied and *so* satisfying. Not only is the *food* good, but you'll be equally impressed with how good *you* feel eating this way, too. Cuisine that is low in fat centers on foods of plant origin. And where food is concerned, that's where the variety is—in the plant world.

Choices are relatively limited—and mostly fatty—at the meat counter and the dairy case. But take a walk through the produce section of your grocery store, or stroll through a farmers' market. The sight is a feast for the senses—so many different shapes, sizes, aromas, textures, flavors, and colors. There are hundreds of varieties of fruits and vegetables. Add to that the enormous number of grains that are available—rice, millet, wheat, oats, barley . . . and then, of course, there are the legumes—lentils, pinto beans, black beans, navy beans . . . the list goes on and on.

So it just takes a trip to the nearest produce stand to see the beauty and abundance of the healthful foods that are right at hand. And that's the best way to describe low-fat, healthful cuisine: beautiful, abundant, delicious, and health-supporting.

Get the Fat Out will help you on your way to a whole new world of food. But a word to the wise: our understanding of human nutrition is evolving rapidly. It's becoming obvious that conventional dietary recommendations are much too conservative to promote significant health benefits, and many times they miss the point altogether.

The current emphasis on reducing fat intake is one example. It's true that most Americans need to cut back on fat. But for the best results, be aware of an even more fundamental change that needs to occur.

As dietary recommendations evolve, there is an increasingly smaller role for animal products in the diet. Plant products such as fruits, vegetables, and whole grains are low in fat and have properties that tend to promote good health. On the other hand, the more animal products the diet contains, the greater the health risks become. So, to get the fat out most effectively, and to promote good health, you need to get the meat and dairy products out, too.

As you work your way through the suggestions in this book, then, you'll need to avoid a potential trap. In their efforts to reduce their fat intake, many people have the tendency to swap one animal product for another. For instance, they may switch from whole milk to skim milk, or they might eat low-fat cheese instead of regular cheese. True, they cut back on fat. But fat isn't the only culprit. It's more than that. Meat and dairy products contain no fiber. They contain cholesterol and too much protein in the amounts that are usually eaten. And the more meat and dairy products the diet includes, the less room there is for health-promoting fruits, vegetables, grains, and legumes. The basic balance of plant to animal products in the diet has to change in order for truly significant health benefits to be had. So get the fat out, but do it most effectively by switching from a diet high in meat and dairy foods to a diet that is plant-based.

With that said, you may now proceed to enjoy this book, bend page corners over, and have fun in your efforts to "get the fat out"!

Suzanne Havala M.S., R.D.
Author, *Simple, Lowfat, & Vegetarian*
coauthor, "position paper of the
American Dietetic Association:
Vegetarian Diets," 1993

INTRODUCTION

■ BY NEAL D. BARNARD, M.D. ■

Millions of Americans want to eat better, knowing it will help us lose weight, feel better, and live longer. But how do we do that with so many demands on our time?

Leaving one set of eating habits behind and heading for another is like treading your way across a swift-running stream: moments of uncertainty, wondering if you'll ever be on solid ground again. Victoria Moran has passed this way before. She is intimately familiar with it, and she knows where the stepping-stones are—hundreds of them. The crossing is easy when you know how, and the other side is a truly great place to be, as she conveys with all the wit and humor for which she is well known.

In one of the most practical guides to nutrition ever published, Victoria Moran provides easy ways to modify recipes and cooking techniques so you can minimize fat and maximize flavor. The results extend far beyond a slender waistline and lower cholesterol. With this book you are equipped with a set of revolutionary tools you can use to modify any recipe, to transform your child's lunch into a healthful feast, to satisfy a family's desire for delicious food while keeping meals 100 percent healthful.

In 1991, Denis Burkitt, M.D., T. Colin Campbell, Ph.D., Oliver Alabaster, M.D., and I presented evidence that our health can be revolutionized to the extent that grains, vegetables, fruits, and legumes displace meat, dairy, and fried foods as our culinary staples. The concept became known as the New Four Food Groups, and has been shown to be an optimal nutritional plan. In 1992, Drs. Larry Scherwitz, Dean Ornish, and I published research showing that making major dietary changes can be accomplished with essentially the same ease as minor changes, and can be much more rewarding. But I soon discovered that we had not had the last word in nutritional advice. Victoria sent me the draft of this book for my review, and I began to test these tips with my patients and with people who attend my lectures. Some are tried-and-true techniques, while others are totally new. But this collection proved to be a treasury for everyone, whatever their background, tastes, or culinary tradition.

I hope you will not only take advantage of these secrets but share them as well. So many of our family members and our friends are trying to cut their cholesterol levels or lose weight. These tips provide a new level of sophistication to the kitchen, the restaurant, or anywhere else you find a plate before you.

Neal Barnard
Author, *Food for Life* and *The Power of Your Plate*

PREFACE

The Facts of Fat

Whether the weakness is for New York cheesecake or country fried chicken, Americans lust after fat even if it kills us—and it often does. We know that fat plays a major role in the number-one killer in the Western world, coronary heart disease. It is also a prime culprit in what may be the number-one nuisance in the Western world, overweight—a term rapidly becoming archaic as the experts tell us that the issue is not *weight* on the scales but *fat* on the body.

High-fat diets have also been indicted as a causative factor in stroke, adult-onset diabetes, gallbladder disorders, high blood pressure, and some types of cancer. The American Cancer Society and the National Cancer Institute recognize one third of all cancers as diet-related. They, along with the American Heart Association and the National Cholesterol Education Program of the National Heart, Lung, and Blood Institute, recommend getting no more than 30 percent of our calories in the form of fat. The American Academy of Pediatrics echoes this recommendation for children over the age of two.

But most of us grew up on Mom's apple pie, Dad's famous steaks, Grandma's gravy, fast-food burgers, and whole milk in the school cafeteria. It's no wonder that the transition from the typical American diet, averaging some 40 percent of calories from fat, to a diet under 30 percent fat can be quite a test.

The challenge is intensified by an ample body of evidence proposing that the 30 percent figure ought to be much lower, that only 20 or 15 or even 10 percent of our calories should come from fat. Then there's the Asian/Mediterranean conflict. It's not a diplomatic issue but rather opposing views as to whether an Asian-style diet—very low in total fat—is superior to a Mediterranean-type diet—moderate in overall fat, with monounsaturated fats predominating.

It can seem so complicated. Few of us really understand what a monounsaturated fat is—or a saturated or polyunsaturated or hydrogenated one for that matter. And if the experts can't agree on how much fat is too much, how are we supposed to make wise choices? And what about cholesterol—the HDL variety we've come to think of as wearing a halo and the LDL sort that we visualize toting a pitchfork?

I didn't feel comfortable attempting to defat my shopping and cooking practices until I'd sorted through all this. Since I was doing free-lance magazine writing on health topics, I was able to interview many physicians and scientists in the forefront of nutritional medicine, who encouraged me to study the scientific journals myself. Although the jargon, the medical mystique, and the sheer numbers of publications were intimidating at first, the information in them was fascinating enough for me to stake out a favorite table and spend one Saturday morning a month at a university medical library.

A recurrent message from those journals is: We can do a great deal to protect ourselves from debilitating diseases three times a day. We can choose whole grains instead of refined ones, add more fresh produce to our daily menus, and demand foods grown without synthetic pesticides. The studies reveal, however, that probably the most important dietary step we can take is to get the fat off our plates to a large degree.

To start to do this, we need to understand a little of the nature of fats and be clear about what it is we're dealing with. The skinny on fats, thirty-second version, is this: we need a small amount of fat to provide our bodies with the essential fatty acids, but most of us get far too much. To begin to reduce your fat intake to below 30 percent of calories, or to the lower amount that you or your doctor believes to be best for you, get some idea of the percentage of calories from fat you consume right now by becoming familiar with the percentage of calories from fat in a few common foods:

asparagus: 6 percent
avocado: 81 percent
banana: 3 percent
beef, ground: 66 percent
butter: 100 percent
cabbage: 7 percent
cheddar cheese: 73 percent
chicken (roasted, white meat, no skin): 19 percent
chicken (roasted, dark meat, no skin): 33 percent
eggs: 65 percent
grapes: 13 percent
lentils: 3 percent
lima beans: 4 percent
milk, low-fat (i.e. 2 percent): 31 percent
milk, whole: 49 percent
oatmeal: 16 percent
potatoes: 1 percent
raisins: less than 1 percent
rice, brown: 5 percent
tuna, oil-packed: 65 percent

> **tuna,** water-packed: 40 percent
> **whole wheat bread:** 8 percent
> *Nutritive Value of American Foods in Common Units,* Agriculture Handbook No. 456.

You can eat a variety of foods throughout the day and keep your percentage of calories from fat at the level you want it. A simple way to achieve this is to concentrate on:

> **whole grains**
> **vegetables**
> **fresh and dried fruits**
> **legumes** (dried beans and peas)
> and **nonfat dairy products** (optional)

In addition to keeping your total fat consumption low, this will guarantee a low intake of cholesterol and of saturated fat, the kind linked most closely to cardiovascular disease. You can further ensure a low fat intake by using cooking and baking methods that do not rely on butter, shortening, margarine, or oil. By doing this, you will be taking positive dietary steps toward reducing your risk of several common degenerative diseases. This style of eating, particularly when combined with aerobic exercise and a healthy mental attitude, is also the preeminent prescription for a lean, lithe body.

Okay, so it was the sixty-second version. If you're in a hurry to get on to the tips and use some of them in tonight's dinner, sixty seconds of background will suffice. If you want to know more of the why before proceeding with the how, stay with me.

UNDERSTANDING FATS

Fats are a vital component of human nutrition. We use fats to manufacture hormones and to provide warmth and stored energy to carry us through in times of famine (and often, much to the chagrin of dieters, in times of self-inflicted deprivation as well). We consume fat that we can see—like butter, margarine, salad oils—and fat that we can't see—the fat in the hamburger, the oil in the peanuts, the shortening in the cake or the piecrust.

Just as our diets need to supply eight essential amino acids to meet our protein needs, the food we eat must provide us with two **essential fatty acids, linoleic** and **linolenic acids.** Because the requirement for these is small—less than fourteen grams a day, the amount in one tablespoon of vegetable oil—most people can meet their fatty acid needs without consuming any foods that are generally thought of as high in fat. It's surprising to learn that even such light fare as apples and broccoli get 6 percent and 15 percent, respectively, of what few calories they do contain from fat, cranberries and kale 13 percent.

Most foods contain a mixture of saturated, monounsaturated, and polyunsaturated fats, but one of these types predominates. **Saturated fats,** found primarily in foods of animal origin and in coconut, cocoa butter, and palm oil, are those held most responsible for coronary heart disease. These fats are solid at room temperature and at body temperature. And these are the fats that encourage the liver to manufacture **cholesterol.**

The animal foods that provide most of the saturated fat Americans consume are also the only source of dietary cholesterol. Cholesterol is necessary for proper hormonal functioning and other physiological processes, and the body conveniently makes all of this substance it can use. That means there is no dietary requirement for it and the excess of both cholesterol and saturated fat in the food we eat accounts in large part for the epidemic of cardiovascular disease in much of the Western world.

Polyunsaturated fats, in vegetable and fish oils, were shown in early studies to lower cholesterol levels in humans. However, more recent research indicates that an excess of oil of any type elevates serum cholesterol since all oils contain some saturated fat. Other studies have demonstrated a link between large amounts of polyunsaturated fats and cancer. Because they increase the development of **free radicals,** unstable molecules that disrupt cellular functioning, polyunsaturates appear to encourage the formation and subsequent growth of tumors. Free radicals are also believed to play a role in instigating the development of the plaque that forms in human arteries.

The plot thickens when polyunsaturated fats sacrifice their characteristic liquid nature and show up solid through the process of **hydrogenation.** To hydrogenate a fat, corn, soy, or some other oil is saturated with hydrogen at the molecular level to harden it to some degree. This is most apparent in the production of margarine, but hydrogenated oils are also found in baked goods, nondairy creamers, many commercial peanut butters, and some ice creams.

This procedure creates compounds known as **trans fatty acids.** The body apparently interprets these as an odd form of saturated fat, raising LDL ("bad" cholesterol) levels (as do naturally saturated fats) but also decreasing the "good" HDLs. Since trans fatty acids are created artificially and hydrogenation is a recent development in human history, we do not yet have the whole story on them. Scientists know enough, however, to discourage the consumption of hydrogenated or partially hydrogenated fats.

Monounsaturated fats, prominent in olive, canola, and

peanut oils, apparently do not cause the wholesale cholesterol elevation of their saturated cousins, nor have they been linked in any conclusive way with cancer. In fact, those populations that consume a reasonably high amount of them—the Greeks, Italians, and Spaniards—have a low incidence of coronary heart disease and less breast cancer than do citizens of the United States, Canada, and the United Kingdom. For this reason, some authorities are telling us to replace much of the saturated and polyunsaturated fat we're cutting out with monounsaturates.

The majority of recommendations at present, however, are to cut down on both saturated fat and total fat consumption. All fats are very high in calories—nine per gram as compared to four per gram for carbohydrates and proteins. Not only does fat carry concentrated calories, but the body likes to hold on to fat from food as body fat. Turning excess carbohydrate calories into storage fat is biochemical hard labor. Since obesity is connected with degenerative illnesses, including hypertension, diabetes, and cancer of the breast, colon, and uterus, eliminating one of its primary causes makes good sense.

In addition, low-fat foods from the plant kingdom abound in the nutritional elements we need—complex carbohydrates, fiber, protein, vitamins, and minerals—while fats provide primarily calories. Indeed, it appears that a truly health-promoting diet not only limits fat, but abounds in vegetables, fruits, and whole grains. For example, compounds found in cabbage family vegetables (cabbage, broccoli, brussels sprouts, cauliflower, etc.) may help discourage cancer formation.

Plant foods are also the source of the antioxidants that can destroy free radicals and as such are believed to be valuable in cancer prevention and forestalling signs of aging. Among these antioxidants are vitamin C (in citrus fruits, tomatoes, peppers, cantaloupe), beta carotene (in carrots, sweet potatoes, yellow squash, and leafy greens), and vitamin E (in green vegetables,

legumes, and whole grains, which also provide another powerful antioxidant, selenium).

HOW MUCH FAT DO WE NEED?

Much fascinating clinical research (comparing a test group
with a control group) and many epidemiological studies (looking at populations and analyzing their incidence of disease)
indicate that very low is very good when it comes to fat intake.
Using breast cancer incidence as an example, the epidemiological testimony is irrefutable that in populations consuming 10
to 15 percent of calories from fat, this disease rarely occurs.

Looking at worldwide breast cancer statistics and fat
consumption on a comparison graph is fascinating because it
illustrates the unmistakable connection between the two.
Women in nations with low-fat diets—countries such as Thai-
land, the Philippines, Taiwan, Sri Lanka, and El Salvador—
have minimal breast cancer. Women living where rich diets
are the norm—in the United States, Canada, Great Britain,
Ireland, New Zealand, the Scandinavian countries, and the
Netherlands—face an alarming probability (one in eight in the
United States) of developing this disease.[1]

There appears to be no genetic component. Groups who
migrate from parts of the world with low cancer rates to those
where cancer is prevalent soon reach the cancer risk rate of their
new country *without any intermarriage taking place.* This is true
not only for breast cancer but for many other types of cancer,
including those affecting the colon, uterus, and prostate.[2]
Environmental influences—and diet is surely among the most
prominent of these—appear to be the deciding factor.

Nevertheless, the headlines that appeared in 1992 following a Harvard study on more than 89,000 American nurses told us that lowering fat intake did not appear to offer protection from breast cancer.[3] This study's subjects on the low-fat end of the spectrum, however, were (according to self-reported dietary surveys) consuming some 27 percent of calories from fat—**not** a low-fat diet by world standards nor optimal according to the latest knowledge. (In 1950s Japan, when breast cancer there was virtually nonexistent, fat intake ranged from 7 to 10 percent of calories.)

When it comes to coronary heart disease, evidence of the efficacy of diets very low in fat is indisputable. The work of Dean Ornish, M.D., at the University of California at San Francisco shows that in persons already suffering from coronary disease, consuming the generally recommended 30 percent of calories from fat actually allows the disease process to continue. However, a 10 percent fat diet with virtually no cholesterol, in concert with moderate exercise and stress management, has enabled the majority of Dr. Ornish's patients to do what was believed to be impossible: reverse atherosclerosis. That is, the plaques of cholesterol and other substances along their artery walls have begun to dissolve.

Other scientific investigations have brought forth similar findings. One was the Framingham Heart Study which followed ten thousand Massachusetts residents over four decades to ascertain what influences are most likely to result in coronary disease. The study's medical director, William Castelli, M.D., has stated, "We've never had a heart attack in Framingham in thirty-five years in anyone who had a cholesterol under 150."[4]

The study showed, however, that for every 1 percent rise in total blood cholesterol over 150 (that is, 150 milligrams of cholesterol per deciliter of blood) came a 2 percent rise in an individual's chance of developing coronary heart disease. This means the standard recommendation in the United States to keep cholesterol levels at under 200 may actually increase coronary risk by 66 percent from the 150 level! A fat intake far below 30 percent of calories appears to be mandatory for most people to achieve and maintain a cholesterol level under 150.

Consuming very little in the way of cholesterol-containing foods (all animal products regardless of their fat content) may also be necessary. "Every 100 mg. of cholesterol you eat in your daily routine adds roughly five points to your cholesterol level. (Everyone is different, and this number is an average.) In practical terms, 100 mg. of cholesterol is four ounces of beef, or four ounces of chicken, or half an egg, or three cups of milk."[5]

When serum cholesterol reaches the 150 level or below, the ratio of HDL ("good") to LDL ("bad") cholesterol loses the importance that it has in persons with higher total readings. **LDLs (low-density lipoproteins)** stimulate development of the plaque that obstructs the arterial walls, while **HDLs (high-density lipoproteins)** have the job of transporting cholesterol out of the arteries. When there is less cholesterol to transport, fewer transport vehicles (HDLs) are produced.

Ornish has reported that his patients eating low-fat, vegetarian diets "have low levels of total cholesterol, very low LDL levels, and very low rates of coronary heart disease *even though their HDL levels tend to be low.* . . ."[6] Even so, the Framingham Study found that vegetarians' total cholesterol to HDL ratio was an ideal 2.9 to 1—better than that of marathon runners.

The most comprehensive nutritional study in humans ever conducted also supports a diet very low in fat. This is the Cornell-China-Oxford Project on Nutrition, Health and Environment, which looked at the eating habits and health status of 6,500 Chinese citizens living in many parts of China.

As in the Framingham study, low serum cholesterol levels were related to a lack of coronary disease, but also to a decreased incidence of cancer and diabetes. "This is pretty remarkable," says the project's Cornell director, nutritional biochemist T. Colin Campbell, Ph.D., "because the plasma cholesterols in rural China are between about 90 and 170 milligrams per deciliter. In other words, their high is our low. What it's really saying in a sense is the lower the cholesterol level the better. High cholesterol levels are related to the consumption of animal foods—and it apparently doesn't take very much of them."[7]

The China study also shed some light on the question of whether or not one can get too little fat in a calorie-sufficient diet. While health professionals debate the comparative merits of a 30 percent fat diet versus a 10 percent fat diet (and all levels in between), the range among subjects in China was 6 to 24 percent—with no apparent ill effects at the lower levels and more degenerative disease occurrence among those with the higher intakes.

SO WHAT DO WE EAT?

The USDA's Food Guide Pyramid is being widely used to replace the archaic Four Food Groups, which did not address the issue of fat at all. The Pyramid exhorts us to consume, on average:

six to eleven servings of grains
five to nine servings of fruits and vegetables
two or three servings of meat, fish, cheese, or legumes
two to three servings of dairy products
minimal use of fats, oils, and sweeteners

This can be used as a basic guide for people who want to eat all the same foods they have traditionally, just in somewhat differing proportions and modified form. To meet the "under 30 percent of calories from fat" guideline, the Pyramid's suggestions would need to be followed along with:

choosing leaner cuts of meat

trimming all visible fat

choosing white meat of poultry and removing the skin

eating smaller portions of meat

having more fish and bean/grain entrees

reducing use of egg yolks

selecting low-fat and nonfat dairy products

Because the 30 percent figure may not provide the margin of safety needed by those prone to coronary disease or otherwise seeking optimal benefits from dietary change, we have the option to improve our diet still more and simplify the process at the same time. This can be done by:

eating the foods that come directly from the earth:

whole grains, vegetables, fruits, and legumes

limiting intake of vegetable oils

using egg whites and nonfat dairy products if desired[8]

This way of eating echoes more closely the recommendations of the China Health Project and those employed by Dr. Dean Ornish with his heart patients. It has been codified in the New Four Food Groups from Physicians Committee for Responsible Medicine:

five or more servings of whole grains

three or more servings of vegetables

two or three servings of legumes or soy products
three or more fruits
other foods if desired as condiments or extras

(The diet Dr. Ornish used in his historic research also allowed up to one-half cup daily of nonfat milk or nonfat yogurt, and egg whites for use in cooking.)

It is possible to create a very low-fat (although not choles-terol-free) diet that includes fish, poultry, and even some lean meat; the highly respected Pritikin program takes this approach. I prefer to stay close to the New Four Food Groups. With few exceptions, the specific foods within these groups are quite low in fat.[9] That means I don't have to count fat grams or calculate percentages; I just eat. And after having agonized through years of dieting, I like the freedom of doing away with portion control and eating until I'm satisfied without worrying about my weight.

Since my basic daily diet is so low in fat—around ten per-cent of calories—I have ample leeway for the occasional splurge without remorse. For example, I make cookies for the holidays and put chopped pecans in them. If I'm ravenous on an airplane and all they give me is peanuts, I eat them. If the nonfat marinara sauce I asked for at the Italian restaurant comes out looking like an oil slick over linguine ("But it's not fat, madam," the waiter assures me, "it's olive oil!"), I can choose to send it back or simply make do. A healthy person on a genuinely low-fat diet can afford an infrequent indiscretion without guilt or remorse.

I also appreciate that the foods in the New Four Food Groups boast a total lack of cholesterol. Coronary disease and dangerously elevated cholesterol levels are common on both sides of my family and, to hear my relatives talk about it, you'd think it had been that way since the Stone Age. Therefore, I prefer to hedge my bets in every way possible. It's evidently working: my cholesterol reading is 138.

And there's nothing complicated about eating like this. I don't need to bother with whatever cholesterol-lowering or protective agent happens to be popular—oat bran one season, fish oil the next. (The oat bran craze ended abruptly when it was learned that any soluble fiber—abundant in beans, for example—produced the same results. And fish oils actually contain substantial saturated fat and cholesterol, as well as potentially harmful environmental contaminants in many cases. Safer sources of omega-3 fatty acids are soy products, garbanzos, wheat, even cauliflower and strawberries.)

Besides, working with vegetables, fruits, whole grains, and legumes is a delightful experience—visually and in a tactile sense. Even the simplest of meals prepared from them can be an exquisite combination of flavors, aromas, and textures. And cleanup is so easy I can't even bring myself to complain about it anymore.

T. Colin Campbell, Ph.D., explained it from a scientist's vantage point when he spoke at a physicians' conference to report on the initial findings of the China Health Project:

> If we are reasonably sure of what our data from these studies are telling us, then why must we be reticent about recommending a diet which we know is safe and healthy? Scientists can no longer take the attitude that the public cannot benefit from information they're not ready for. We must have the integrity to tell them the truth and let them decide what to do with it. We cannot force them to follow the guidelines we recommend, but we can give them these guidelines and then let them decide. I personally have great faith in the public. We must tell them that a diet of roots, stems, seeds, flowers, fruit, and leaves is the healthiest diet and the only diet we can promote, endorse, and recommend.[10]

I agree. (I also like the way he describes the food. It reminds me of botany class.) I understand, however, that major changes take major motivation. "Some habits," wrote Mark Twain, "must be eased downstairs a step at a time." How we choose to do that easing and to what degree are personal decisions. That's why some transitional tips are included on the pages that follow. Surprisingly, though, going further than we think we're up for may be easier than we anticipate.

A study conducted by Dr. Ornish and Dr. Neal Barnard on the acceptability of low-fat diets found that people on a fat-reduced regimen with chicken and fish and a fat content around 30 percent reacted almost identically to those on a vegetarian program with about 10 percent fat. Both found their new diets somewhat limiting initially ("All that chicken and fish!" "All those grains and beans!"), but they found new ways to prepare the foods and came to enjoy their respective ways of eating.[11]

This doesn't mean they came out even: the group on the 10 percent fat regimen were getting what they came for—marked reduction in their cholesterol levels and the clearing of their perilously clogged arteries. The other group, although tolerating their dietary change equally well, did not experience any profound improvement in their health. As stated earlier, the coronary blockages among these people actually became more pronounced.

It's discouraging to make an effort and not be rewarded with results. But when you can trust that what you're doing can, according to an impressive volume of scientific evidence, improve your chances for a long, healthy life, adopting a new dietary style seems far less onerous. And when you understand how, without dieting or deprivation, eating nature's low-fat foods can keep you as trim as you were in the high school yearbook at your twentieth—or fiftieth—class reunion, you'll want to make the changes.

We've so long viewed high-fat foods as desirable—we even call them "rich"—that the idea of doing without them much of the time can seem like culinary impoverishment. But that's only true if we don't know how to choose the highest quality low-fat foods we're able to pay for and prepare them in tasty, creative ways—the ways you'll learn in this book.

Low-fat cooking can reveal all the virtuosity the cordon bleu kind ever did. It can also be a means of approaching food that is easy, accessible to even the least chef-like among us, and in many cases as quick as cruising past the drive-through window—well, at least as quick as cruising past the drive-through window at noon on a Saturday. And even when you choose to invest more time in your low-fat feasts, if they're adding years to your life, what's a few extra minutes in the kitchen?

REFERENCES

■ THE FACTS OF FAT ■

1. A chart showing this appears on page 83 of *The McDougall Plan* by John A. McDougall, M.D. (Hampton, N.J.: New Win Publishers, 1984).

2. T. Colin Campbell, Ph.D., lecture, Iowa State University, Ames, October 1992.

3. This study was reported in the *Journal of the American Medical Association*, vol. 268, no. 15, Oct. 21, 1992, in "Dietary Fat and Fiber in Relation to Risk of Breast Cancer: An 8-Year Follow-Up," by W. C. Willet, D. J. Hunter, M. J. Stampfer, and others.

4. William Castelli, M.D., quoted in *The Power of Your Plate* by Neal Barnard, M.D. Summertown, Tenn.: The Book Publishing Co., 1990, p. 15.

5. Neal Barnard, M.D., *Food for Life*. New York: Harmony Books, 1993, p. 36.

6. Dean Ornish, M.D., *Dr. Dean Ornish's Program for Reversing Heart Disease*. New York: Random House, 1991, pp. 269–70.

7. T. Colin Campbell, Ph.D., interviewed by author.

8. There is controversy over whether or not cow's-milk products should be recommended. They do provide certain useful nutrients—calcium, riboflavin, vitamin B12—but they are not the only sources of these. Dairy products' high protein concentration (particularly in the fat-reduced varieties); their high allergenic potential; their cholesterol content; the possible

connection between one of their breakdown products, galactose, and ovarian cancer; and a proposed link between the protein found in cow's milk and juvenile diabetes have concerned some experts. Cow's-milk products have also been indicted as a causative factor in iron deficiency anemia, particularly in children.

The books of John McDougall, M.D. (*The McDougall Plan, The McDougall Program,* and others listed in the Bibliography), argue persuasively against the regular use of dairy foods, and they provide ample references to the scientific literature which support that view. In this book, nonfat dairy foods are included with a nondairy alternative given. Often these alternatives are based on soy and therefore contain more fat than the dairy choices that are available in nonfat forms. This amount of fat is fully acceptable in the diet of anyone consuming no animal products and a minimum of extracted vegetable oils. (Total vegetarians need to obtain a reliable source of vitamin B12 after three years on the diet or if pregnant or nursing.)

9. There are a few foods in the New Four Food Groups which have moderate or high concentrations of fat. Avocado, for example, is a fruit that is very high in fat. Soy beans, in the legume group, have 40 percent of their calories from fat, but when used in reasonable quantities with other, lower-fat foods, soy products can be a valuable part of the diet, especially for vegetarians. (There is even research indicating that soy bean consumption may play a part in breast cancer prevention.) When a person is healthy and eating a truly low-fat diet, these foods and other rich plant foods such as nuts can be used in reasonable quantities for dietary diversity and to meet the exceptionally high caloric needs of some individuals.

10. T. Colin Campbell, Ph.D., from an address to the First National Conference for the Elimination of Coronary Artery Disease, November 1991, Phoenix; quoted by Charles Attwood, M.D., in interview with author.

11. This work was reported in the *Journal of Cardiopul-monary Rehabilitation,* vol. 12, no. 6, November/December 1992: "Adherence and Acceptability of a Low-Fat, Vegetarian Diet Among Patients with Cardiac Disease," by Neal D. Barnard, M.D., Larry W. Scherwitz, Ph.D., and Dean Ornish, M.D.

CHAPTER 1

Get the Fat Out
of Your Kitchen

A great many fat-cutting tips are of the multiuse variety: they apply to breakfast, lunch, and dinner, and they can be utilized time and again until they become habits. They can even start family traditions.

Have you heard the old story about the bride who cut the ends off the roast every time she cooked one? When her husband asked her why, she realized she was simply doing what her mother had done. She asked her mother the reason for the practice and was told, "I don't know. Ask your grandmother." Grandma didn't know either and sent her to Great-grandmother's house. Great-grandmother said, "When I married your great-grandfather, we had only one small roasting pan. A roast never fit in it, so I started cutting off the end." The rest is history, or at least hearsay.

The point is, when you serve your family low-fat meals, you're defining "normal" for your children when it comes to food. And you're defining it in a healthy way. It's likely then that they'll feed their children this way, too—and on and on. People have cheated, stolen, and lied for less immortality than that.

So we'll begin with these—the fundamental fat-busters, the basics on degreasing your grocery cart, your kitchen cabinets, and the way you prepare food. Start slowly if that feels right. Try one or two of the suggestions. Work with them and get comfortable.

Give yourself plenty of credit. I knew I was making progress when the quart of imported olive oil I'd bought at my favorite Italian market was more than half full when I went back there six weeks later. Before, I'd have gone through all of it in a month and been using the bottle as a candle holder. Look for your fat-trimming successes and celebrate each one.

(Remember the notations on some of the tips that are used throughout this book: *mod.* indicates items to be used sparingly due to their higher fat content; *inter.* indicates intermediate or transitional tips to help you toward a way of eating that incorporates fewer animal products and more high-fiber complex carbohydrates and vitamin-rich plant foods.)

TASTEFUL TECHNIQUES

1. ■ **The very easiest way to cut fat is to stop *adding* it** to other foods—oily dressings on salad, butter or margarine on bread, greasy gravy on mashed potatoes.

2. ■ **Develop fear of frying.** Frying makes any food a fatty food, and heating oils to the smoking point is believed to cause rampant free-radical production. In addition, there is evidence that cancer-causing chemicals form when food is charred. So donate your deep-fryer to the neighborhood rummage sale and don't look back. Instead look to the many fat-moderating cooking techniques you have to choose from:

3. ▪ **Steaming.** This is especially good for guaranteeing bright, slightly crunchy vegetables and it leaves the bulk of their vitamins intact. If you eat fish *(inter.)*, that may be steamed as well. And leftovers can be reheated by steaming.

4. ▪ **Boiling.** If you boil vegetables, keep the cooking time to a minimum and save the water for soup stock.

5. ▪ **Stewing.** Allow plenty of time for flavors to mingle.

6. ▪ **Baking.** You can use a nonstick pan or nonstick cooking spray to avoid greasing a baking dish.

7. ▪ **Pressure cooking.** "Pressure-cooking gives 2-hour taste in 10 minutes," says Lorna Sass, the world's leading authority on the technique. "Since fat is used to carry flavor, you can eliminate it and let the pressure cooker perform that function. Fat-free soups and stews done in a pressure cooker taste incredibly rich." For more on this, see Sass's book, *Cooking Under Pressure*.

8. ▪ **Microwaving.** A microwave is a timesaver for busy people and nullifies the need for adding fat. The microwave is also useful for warming leftovers.

▪ BONUS TIP: *Until more research is done on the possibility of unsafe substances leaking from plastic containers into food microwaved in them, the conservative course is to use glass or Corning Ware for your microwave cooking and glass or wax paper covers.*

9. ▪ **Roasting.** Roast with a rack if you're cooking meat *(inter.)*. Vegetables can also be roasted and it gives them a cookout quality even vegetable-snubbing children can't resist (see tip 302).

10. ▪ **Oven-"frying" for breaded foods.** Place your breaded food on a nonstick cookie sheet and bake (at about 400 degrees for most things), turning if necessary for even browning.

11. ▪ **Stir-frying.** Use a small amount of oil the way skilled Asian chefs do, and stir nonstop so the food is quickly seared. (Tip 299 gives detailed instructions for a never-fail vegetable stir-fry.) *Mod.*

12. ▪ **Pseudo-sautéing.** This is similar to stir-frying but takes a bit longer as you're depending on the foods' natural moisture to assist in the cooking process. Begin with the tiniest quantity of oil and add water as needed—about 2 tablespoons at a time—to provide additional moisture.

Chef Ron Pickarski states in his cookbook, *Friendly Foods,* that adding a little salt will help extract moisture from vegetables so you can wait to add water until near the end of cooking and you can use less of it. (*Use extreme caution every time you add water to hot oil. There will be a puff of steam and a possible splatter when the water hits the pan.*) If you want a drier result, keep the pan uncovered and use minimal water; for a wet dish, add extra water, cover, and let steaming finish the cooking process.

13. ▪ **Oven-sautéing.** Set your oven at 400 to 425 degrees and place vegetables in a pan covered with nonstick cooking spray (use the spray even if you have a nonstick pan; it will give the veggies more of a sautéed quality). Remove from the oven when they're softened.

14. ▪ **Water-sautéing.** The technical term for this is steeping. Heat the water first unless you're doing onions, which get tender faster when started in cold water. The more thinly you chop your veggies, the more quickly and evenly they'll cook. Make a water-sauté zingier by adding the juice of a lime and some high-quality tamari soy sauce (try the ones flavored with ginger or mushrooms). Experiment with the following oil-free sauté liquids and discover your favorites. The stronger-flavored items need to be added to water; the others can stand on their own:

15. ▪ **Vegetable broth**—saved from cooking vegetables, mixed from an instant broth powder, or homemade stock (see tips 172, 173, and 174).

16. ■ Tomato juice or regular or low-sodium V-8.
17. ■ Lemon juice.
18. ■ Vinegar—try balsamic, rice, wine, and apple cider vinegars.
19. ■ Sherry or another red or white wine.
20. ■ Worcestershire sauce.
21. ■ Barbecue sauce.
22. ■ Fruit juice—apple, orange, or grape, especially appropriate for sautéing the onions and garlic you'll use in a lentil or rice dish.
23. ■ Use a lower heat setting when sautéing with less oil.
24. ■ Stir—let elbow grease replace cooking with grease.
25. ■ Since water, broth, and juice evaporate quickly at cooking temperatures, use enough liquid and keep a close watch. Leaving your scallions and shallots alone while you answer the phone or feed the dog can both cost you the scallions and shallots and let you know your smoke alarm works. I can vouch for this because I've done it more than once.

   ■ BONUS TIP: *If you cook a pot dry and end up with a burned spot, clean the pot as usual, then put about 2 inches of water in it and add 2 or 3 tablespoons of baking soda. Let it sit overnight. This is virtually foolproof.*

26. ■ Pureed starches thicken just about anything from pâtés to soups to sauces. You can puree cooked dried beans or pasta, or use mashed potato for this purpose. (A restaurant in the forefront of light cuisine, Milly's Healthful Gourmet Dining in San Rafael, California, earned wide acclaim for succulent pâtés based on raw cashews. They're now making the same pâtés using fat-negligible potatoes. Their reputation for succulent pâtés continues—and not a single patron noticed when they made the switch.)

27. ■ Experiment with chopping and slicing techniques.

Cooking with less fat provides the opportunity to learn how the thickness or thinness of various foods affects a dish.

■ BONUS TIP: *Combine foods by texture as well as by taste and color. Strive for at least a few different textures in each meal.*

28. ■ **Use lots of moist ingredients** in cooking to make up for the oily moistness you might be missing. Virginia Messina, M.P.H., R.D., suggests adding pineapple to stir-fries and bean dishes, and plumped raisins (i.e., raisins soaked in water for a few hours before using) to curry dishes.

TOOLS OF THE TRADE

29. ■ **Invest in *good* nonstick cookware.** If you're forever scraping off a cheap coating and food is sticking to the pan, it's easy to take the path of least resistance and go back to butter. One quality nonstick line is Millennium from Farberware—you can use metal utensils on this and it still carries a lifetime guarantee, no questions asked. Another is Analon. With thick copper bottoms and durable nonstick coating, these pans can be used to "fry" potatoes without oil and even reheat cooked rice without additional water.

30. ■ **Use heavy pans** if you don't have nonstick cookware. You're less likely to have food stick when the pot it's in has some substance to it.

31. ■ **Those indestructible iron pots** can be made virtually nonstick by rubbing them with coarse salt. Rub in the salt, covering the bottom of the pan. Then turn over the pan, spilling out the salt. The "powder" remaining on the bottom helps make the pot "nonstick." (George Eisman, R.D., who gave me this tip, also reminded me that people on low-sodium diets will need to skip this one. They can still use iron pots, although the pots do need to be periodically "seasoned" with solid shortening. Anyone who doesn't have iron pots can toss out that shortening in a dramatic kitchen fat-purge.)

32. ▪ **A wok is helpful** for preparing stir-fry dishes with a minimum of oil: its shape allows the oil (or other cooking liquid) to settle at the bottom so it's easy to keep it in contact with the food. Nonstick woks can be found at the better department stores and many discount stores as well. (I especially enjoy my nonstick electric wok; it cooks without heating up my kitchen and is a snap to clean.)

33. ▪ **A stainless steel steaming rack** is inexpensive and opens up a world of healthful culinary possibilities. Many aware cooks opt for bamboo steaming baskets found in cookware departments and import shops. Electric steamer/rice cooker combinations are popular among low-fat gourmets as well. They promise top-of-the-line results and easy cleaning.

34. ▪ **Purchase the best knives your budget will allow.** Low-fat, high-fiber food preparation means lots of chopping and slicing, so your knives should be of high-carbon stainless steel and have handles that feel good and fit your hand. Have your knives sharpened at least once a year and try to remember to use a sharpening steel every time you use a knife to help it keep its edge. Washing knives by hand instead of in the dishwasher should help maintain sharpness, too.

35. ▪ **Kitchen scissors** get more use when you're fixing low-fat, natural foods. You'll use them for chopping fresh herbs, citrus segments, and dried fruits. (I adore my stainless steel Oxo Good Grips kitchen shears—and they're designed to work for left-handed people as well as for right-handed ones.)

36. ▪ **A food processor** is not a necessity of life, but if you've been thinking of getting one (or if the one you've got is on some high shelf gathering dust), getting the fat out of your diet may be the impetus you need. This machine can make short work of slicing and grating, and it's also valuable in blending the ingredients for fat-free purees and sauces.

37. ■ **You may as well have a blender, too,** for shakes and smoothies and the like. That blender in the neighbors' garage sale will do, but if you're a serious cook and entertain a lot, you may want to consider a heavy duty model. The Vita-Mix (a powerful blender-juicer that does a lot of other things as well) fits the bill here, as does the Oster Professional Blender.

SUPERMARKET SAVVY

38. ■ **Use the finest and freshest ingredients available.** If fat is supposed to carry flavor and you're not using it, the genuine taste of your foods and seasonings will have to carry themselves. Yellow broccoli and limp celery won't do it.

39. ■ **Shop for your basics from the New Four Food Groups:** whole grains, vegetables, fruits, and legumes. Think of other foods as condiments, flavorings, or for occasional use.

40. ■ **Indulge yourself with gourmet treats** that don't add appreciable fat: fine Dijon mustard, raspberry and tarragon vinegars, capers, fresh herbs. Such additions can add delightfully to the taste appeal of a dish and they can make you feel affluent for a lot less than a Mercedes.

41. ■ **Add fiber so there's no room for fat.** Use beans and lentils in casseroles, soups, stews, dips. (As a bonus, the fiber in these foods has been shown to aid in lowering cholesterol levels.)

42. ▪ **Starchy chestnuts and water chestnuts** can substitute for oily nuts in side dishes and vegetarian entrees.

▪ BONUS TIP: *How do you feel about that word "starchy"? Unless you're very young, starch may still sound like something to avoid. But starch—complex carbohydrate—comprises the greatest part of a healthy diet. Practice saying "Starch is good; I can eat all I want."*

43. ▪ **Nonfat milk** can replace whole milk in recipes and on cereal. If you prefer to avoid dairy products, you can find at health food stores low-fat Rice Dream, a milklike drink made from rice, and low-fat soy milks (technically called "soy beverages").

44. ▪ **Plain nonfat yogurt** is a versatile stand-in for sour cream and heavy cream. Make sure its only ingredients are skim milk and yogurt cultures; fillers and extenders won't give you the results you're after. Soy yogurt, not yet available in fat free form, is still reasonably low in fat (the flavored kinds have less fat than the plain) and makes a satisfactory nondairy alternative.

45. ▪ **Butter Buds Butter Flavored Mix can be found at any supermarket** and give that buttery taste you might be missing with no fat. Mixed with hot tap water, they make a liquid melted butter flavoring. The granules may also be sprinkled on hot foods or stirred into soups or mashed potatoes.

46. ▪ **Imitation butter flavoring** (with the vanilla and other extracts at the supermarket) works, too. Although it's totally fat free, it's not a natural product, so I don't recommend it for everyday use.

47. ▪ **Coconut lovers can get a touch of that distinctive flavor** and a whiff of the wonderful scent with coconut extract or (*mod.*) fat-reduced coconut milk with some three-quarters less fat than it would have otherwise. (One brand is A Taste of Thai.) Or you can just use coconut shampoo, lather vigorously, and imagine. . . .

SPICING LIFE

48. ▪ **Fats are seen as flavor enhancers, so enhance in other ways** by using garlic, ginger, mustard, onion, flavored vinegars, piquant citrus juices and zest, and surprising herbs like fennel and cilantro. Feel free to double up on these when you're not using oil or butter.

49. ▪ **Don't even think of using ordinary salt and pepper** in your low-fat dishes. Freshly ground pepper and salt ground from crystals in your own table mill make a tremendous difference. (Adding salt after cooking gives its full impact so you needn't use as much.)

▪ BONUS TIP: *In India (where old wives' tales are actually ancient), it's said that if you put the salt you plan to use in the palm of your hand and smell it before adding it to your dish, you'll know instinctively whether you have the right amount or if you need a bit more or less.*

50. ▪ **Try real Japanese tamari or shoyu** instead of ordinary soy sauce, which often adds only saltiness (and often some artificial preservative) to your food instead of rich tenor. To be dictionary-accurate, shoyu contains wheat; tamari doesn't. They're both aged to develop their distinctive quality and aroma, and both come in regular and salt-reduced forms at natural food stores. If you're a supermarket shopper, the Kikkoman soy sauces, regular and low sodium, are very good.

51. ▪ **A nutmeg grinder** belongs on your table right next to (or even instead of) those for salt and pepper. Fresh nutmeg is an unexpectedly versatile condiment to perk up all your fat-free fare.

▪ BONUS TIP: *Gourmet chefs prefer whole spices. You can buy whole and grind many spices—cloves, cumin, coriander, fennel seed, star anise.*

52. ■ **When you buy dried herbs and spices,** get the youngest ones you can so they'll give the most intense flavor to your low-fat dishes. If you're lucky enough to live in a city with an herb and spice shop, that's probably the best place for these. Get the smallest practical quantity and store in an airtight container so the essence of the herb or spice will be there when you want it. Alternatively, if you belong to a food co-op or buying club, you can buy spices and herbs in bulk and freeze the excess.

53. ■ **Get a spice chart for your kitchen** and match specific herbs and flavoring agents to the foods with which each one works best:

> *basil* for tomatoes, potatoes, cucumber, squash
> *caraway seeds* for beets, cabbage, potatoes, rye bread
> *garlic* for string beans, mushrooms, beans, tomatoes, greens
> *lemon juice* for asparagus, broccoli, spinach, salads
> *savory* for beans, peas, lentils, salads, and vegetable juices

■ BONUS TIP: *Fresh herbs pack a tangy punch hard to match with dried ones. Growing an herb garden is uncomplicated and fun, indoors or out. Basil, parsley, chives, and dill are especially easy to grow. Most recipes expect you to use dried herbs; just double the amount for fresh.*

54. ■ **Edible flowers** add not just grace and beauty to your table, but they often lend a wondrous taste to the dish they're garnishing as well. At my house, we like spicy nasturtiums, lovely scarlet runner blossoms, delicate violets, romantic rose petals, and prolific edible marigolds. (For more ideas, see *Cooking with Flowers* by Jenny Leggatt.)

55. ■ **Hot sauce on practically anything** gives your taste buds so much to think about they won't know you're cutting fat.

56. ■ **Pungent curries have the same quality.** My friend Susan, who looks after my kitties when I travel, never felt satisfied eating low-fat foods until she volunteered to spend a week cooking for a visiting dignitary from India. "The spices really got my attention," she says. "The food filled me up quicker and I felt full longer." You can make your own Indian spice blend from ground ginger, cumin, cinnamon, mustard powder, cayenne, and turmeric. Experiment with proportions until you find the combination that makes you feel like a maharajah.

57. ■ **Spice pastes are superb additions to Indian cuisine.** Commercial brands of curry paste and the unique, flavorful biryani paste are available at ethnic and gourmet shops. Most do contain some oil, but chef Michael Forsberg has provided these instructions for making your own oil-free spice paste:

■ **SPICY SPICE PASTE** ■

$1/2$ small onion
$1/2$-inch knob peeled ginger
2 to 3 garlic cloves, peeled
$1/2$ teaspoon whole coriander seed
$1/4$ teaspoon whole cumin seed
$1/8$ teaspoon whole fennel seed
1 or 2 serrano or jalapeño peppers (if you want a hot paste)
$1/2$ cup water

Blend all ingredients in a blender until smooth. (The peppers are optional; if you want to be middle of the road on spiciness, use them but remove their seeds.) When you use this in a recipe, cook until the water evaporates—the spices aren't roasted so they must be cooked. This is enough spice paste to season a curry for 4 to 6 people. Use immediately or store refrigerated for no longer than one month. ■

58. ■ **Fat-free marinades** are priceless for imparting savor to beans, tofu, vegetables, and anything else you might want to grill. Many of the same liquids used as sautéing alternatives (fruit or vegetable juice, broth, vinegar, diluted soy sauce, wine) may also be used in marinades. A basic marinade combines 3 cups of apple juice and 2 cloves of pressed garlic with 1 cup of tamari soy sauce or Bragg's Liquid Aminos (an unfermented form of soy sauce that many people prefer; it's sold at health food stores).

59. ▪ **Discover extracts** for subtle ambience in your foods. Try almond, banana, lemon, rum, peppermint. If you prefer to avoid alcohol, look for natural flavorings preserved without alcohol at your natural foods store or spice shop. (Instead of using vanilla in extract form, I sometimes use chopped fresh vanilla bean—good in recipes requiring a blender—or fragrant vanilla powder from a spice or gourmet shop.)

THE FINE ART OF MODERATION

60. ▪ **Pare the amounts** of eggs, butter, margarine, mayonnaise, and oil by a third or half. This rarely harms a recipe and it's sure to benefit your body. *Inter./Mod.*

▪ BONUS TIP: *Congratulate yourself on little things while realizing they're just the beginning. Even something as minuscule as using one pat of butter on toast instead of two results in a savings of four grams of fat every time you do it. Don't lull yourself into thinking this alone can make any real difference in either your health or your measurements, but if you have the luxury of giving yourself some time to change, every step in the right direction brings you nearer your goal.*

61. ▪ **If you feel you need to add butter, oil, or margarine** to a cooked dish, do it just before serving so the flavors won't be "cooked away" and weakened. *Mod.*

62. ▪ **Olive, canola, and peanut oils are the preferred choices,** because of their monounsaturated fat content. Extra-virgin olive oil, from the first pressing, is considered best—and quality is paramount when you're using very small quantities. *Mod.*

63. ▪ **Be aware of amounts any time you cook with oil.** Even the monounsaturates should never be used by the cup or any fraction of it. There are 13.6 grams of fat in every tablespoon of extracted oil, so gauge it as you do extracts or spices, by the measuring spoon. *Mod.*

64. ▪ **For an oil sauté,** cut the amount by putting the oil in an already heated skillet. A little oil goes further that way and the food absorbs less of it than it would if you'd started with cold oil. *Mod.*

65. ▪ **You needn't cover the bottom of the pan with oil to sauté or stir-fry.** Just put the food where the oil is—at the edges of the frying pan or the bottom of the wok. And keep the onion, garlic, or whatever you're cooking *moving* with chopsticks or a spatula. *Mod.*

66. ▪ **Toasted sesame oil** has such a strong savor that a few *drops* can make a noteworthy impact on many dishes, particularly those with an Asian flair. *Mod.*

67. ▪ **Learn the chef's trick of infusion.** Let fresh herbs make a home in a bottle of oil; then even the smallest amounts of oil will carry a heady flavor. *Mod.*

68. ▪ **When you use olives,** use one per person instead of a half or whole cup per recipe. Mince the olives finely and use some of the juice for taste. The juice is quite salty—that's why they call it brine—but it imparts a lot of flavor without the fat of the olives themselves. *Mod.* (This comes from cookbook author Margaret Malone, co-owner of Milly's Healthful Gourmet Dining, San Rafael.)

69. ▪ **Replacing extracted oils with ground nuts and**

seeds works in a variety of recipes—dressings, sauces, soups, even desserts. This trick is used often by chef Ron Pickarski, a gold medalist in the International Culinary Olympics. The substantial fat content of the nuts and seeds—which, of course, needs to be taken into account when you plan the meal as a whole—will give the "mouth feel" you're looking for without using a refined oil. *Mod.*

70. ■ **Know rich foods when you see them.** They don't have to be out of your life forever and ever. Simply relegate them to the class of "rich relatives"—the ones you see on birthdays and special occasions. It's nice when you get together but you wouldn't want to do it every day. *Mod., of course.*

CHAPTER 2

Get the Fat Out of
Bread and Breakfast

Breakfast is my favorite meal, probably because morning is my favorite time. The day is just waiting there, full of possibilities, and it is profoundly pleasant to ponder them while I sip my tea. I realize that this fondness for the early hours is not universal: You may prefer breakfast on the run, or no breakfast at all. Most books about better eating would say, "For shame!" I say, "Trust your instincts. If you're treating yourself to good food, I don't believe it's anybody's business when you eat it."

Many foods we associate with breakfast—whether eaten early, late, as a Sunday brunch, or as a casual supper on Saturday night—can be as healthful as they are comforting. Fruits and breads, the basis of a classic continental breakfast, can come to your table as lean as can be. Ditto for hot and cold cereals.

Unfortunately, in spite of the fact that most Americans work in fairly sedentary occupations, it is not difficult to chow down a morning meal as if we've been splitting rails since dawn and are about to hitch up the team to plow the back forty. Rich, heavy breakfasts are a throwback, but if you were to snoop in any coffee shop or diner tomorrow morning, you would see plenty of our friends and neighbors greeting the day with bacon and eggs, biscuits and gravy, or pancakes made with whole eggs and whole milk and about to be topped with a mini-Matterhorn of butter.

Even many who believe they eat lightly in the morning are having a doughnut or croissant or one of those fast-food sandwiches with egg, cheese, and ham. These breakfasts are light when weighed on a scale, but they're heavy on fat nonetheless. There are many better ways to breakfast that keep fat down and energy soaring. The tips in this chapter will help you do just that. And the ideas for breads, of course, can be recycled for lunch and dinner.

BREADS AND SPREADS

71. ■ **Eat your bread unadorned** like the elegant French, or with a bit of olive oil *(mod.)* like the healthy-hearted Italians.

72. ■ **Whole grain breads aren't just noble,** they also have enough flavor and texture to taste good on their own, far better butterless than white or mostly white breads.

73. ■ **Pita, French, and sourdough breads** are by definition virtually fat free. Sourdough is a doubly good deal because anyone who really likes it doesn't care to hide that pleasing sourness under butter or margarine.

74. ■ **Having corn bread for breakfast** lets anyone be an honorary Southerner, at least until lunchtime. Jennifer Raymond's lovely cookbook, *The Peaceful Palate: Fine Vegetarian Cuisine,* provides the low-fat, cholesterol-free corn bread recipe I use most often:

■ CORN BREAD ■

$1^1/_2$ cups soy milk
$1^1/_2$ tablespoons vinegar
1 cup cornmeal
1 cup flour (unbleached white or whole wheat pastry)
2 tablespoons raw sugar or other sweetener
$^3/_4$ teaspoon salt
1 teaspoon baking powder
$^1/_2$ teaspoon baking soda
2 tablespoons oil

Preheat oven to 425 degrees. Combine soy milk and vinegar
and let stand. Mix dry ingredients in a large bowl. Add the soy
milk mixture and the oil and stir until just blended. Spread the
batter evenly in a greased 9 × 9-inch baking dish, and bake at
425 degrees for 25 to 30 minutes. Serve hot. *Serves 8.* ■

75. ■ **Home-baked yeast breads don't really require fat,**
even when the recipe calls for it.

76. ■ **If you want that bit of moistness oil provides** in the
bread you bake, use some regular soy milk as part of the liquid
called for. My friend Kate in Denver, a masterful baker, does
this all the time and gets the richness oil would impart with far
less fat.

■ BONUS TIP: *Any bread tastes best when you chew it very*
well. That's because the enzymes to start its digestion are secreted in
the mouth. When you chew it thoroughly, the starches break down
into sugars and the bread tastes superb.

77. ■ **Sprouted wheat bread is naturally sweet** because the
germination process does much of the starch breakdown for
you. Baked at low temperatures, these solid, round loaves
are made from 100 percent sprouted wheat—no flour, oil, or

sweeteners. Find them in the freezer at most health food stores. Brand names include Essene Bread from Lifestream Natural Foods or Manna Bread from Nature's Path. They're exquisitely dessertlike, especially the kinds with cinnamon and raisins or carrots and dates added.

78. ▪ Bran muffins sound innocent, but bagels are often a better bet. Unless you're sure your muffin, bran or not, was made without egg yolks and ample shortening, choose the bagel. If you get a cinnamon-raisin one, it's easy to forgo the cream cheese. (Fat-reduced cream cheese is on the market, both dairy and soy varieties. Check the package for amount of fat.)

79. ▪ You can find low-fat muffins, too—everywhere from fast-food restaurants to natural food stores and supermarkets (Health Valley Fat-Free Muffins are available at the latter two places).

80. ▪ Or bake your own muffins with no added fat. This recipe comes from *Ecological Cooking: Recipes to Save the Planet,* by Joanne Stepaniak and Kathy Hecker.

▪ CHUNKY APPLE SPICE MUFFINS ▪

Dry ingredients

    2 cups whole wheat flour
    2 teaspoons baking powder
    1 teaspoon arrowroot powder
    $1/_2$ teaspoon allspice
    2 teaspoons cinnamon
    $1/_4$ teaspoon ground cloves
    $1/_4$ teaspoon powdered ginger

Wet ingredients

    $1/_2$ cup sorghum syrup or natural fruit syrup
    $1/_2$ cup unsweetened applesauce

2 tart apples, peeled and diced small
$^{1}/_{2}$ cup water
$^{1}/_{2}$ teaspoon vanilla extract

Mix dry ingredients and wet ingredients separately. Pour wet ingredients into dry and mix thoroughly. Spoon into prepared muffin tins (preferably nonstick) and bake at 400 degrees for about 25 minutes. *Makes 12 large muffins.* ■

81. ■ Spread your bread (or muffin or roll or what have you) with jam—the all-fruit jams and conserves taste like concentrated summer.

82. ■ Or drizzle on honey.

83. ■ Or a dollop of nonfat or soy yogurt.

84. ■ Or real Vermont maple syrup.

85. ■ You can make a nonfat "butter" yourself, and you don't need a churn, just a double boiler. This method comes from Honolulu culinary instructor Elaine French:

■ **CORNY BUTTER** ■

$^{1}/_{4}$ cup corn flour
1 cup water
$^{1}/_{2}$ teaspoon salt
1 tablespoon Emes gelatin plus cold water to soften

Stir the corn flour, water, and salt together in the top of a double boiler. Cook slowly until thick. Then dissolve gelatin in cold water to soften it and heat the gelatin-water mixture briefly as you would for a gelatin salad or dessert. Add the gelatin liquid to the corn flour mixture and stir to combine. Refrigerate to set. This positively *melts* on hot toast. ■

(Note: Corn flour is very finely ground cornmeal. It should be available at your natural foods store. Emes gelatin is available at both natural foods stores and kosher markets. If you can't find it, use agar flakes from the health food store or, if you aren't vegetarian, unflavored gelatin from the supermarket.)

86. ■ **A butterlike spread with no hydrogenated oils** and very little saturated fat is Spectrum Spread from Spectrum Naturals, Petaluma, California, sold in natural foods stores. Made from canola oil, this is pure fat, as is butter or margarine, but its fatty acid profile is far superior to either of these. Thickeners (xanthum and guar gums and soy protein isolate) replace hydrogenation. (We'd done fine at our house for years with no oily spreads at all, but discovering this one allowed me to resurrect my favorite childhood breakfast: cinnamon toast. I use the barest bit of Spectrum Naturals Spread and dust on brown sugar and cinnamon—umm.) *Mod.*

TOASTS AND TOPPERS

87. ■ **Thickened cherries** are a colorful and delicious topping for toast or pancakes. This recipe comes from *Ten Talents,* by Rosalie Hurd and Frank Hurd, D.C., M.D.:

■ THICKENED CHERRIES ■

1 cup fruit juice or water
2 tablespoons arrowroot powder
1 quart pitted cherries (or thaw frozen, unsweetened
    cherries; they're already pitted)
$1/3$ cup honey

Pinch of salt
Dash of lemon juice

Thicken juice or water over medium heat with arrowroot, stirring so it won't get lumpy. Add cherries, honey, salt, and lemon juice. Heat till warmed through. (You may thicken other fruit the same way.) ▪

88. ▪ **Beans on toast** is a British staple, and it makes a robust breakfast on either side of the Atlantic. Heating leftover or canned vegetarian baked beans makes this hot meal in no time.

89. ▪ **Creamed corn** dresses up toast becomingly, too, in the morning or any other time of day. Don't let the "cream" in this suggestion scare you; you can make nonfat creamed corn in your blender. Freya Dinshah, author of *The Vegan Kitchen*, taught me how:

▪ CREAMED CORN ▪

6 cups corn, fresh or frozen
$1^1/_2$ cups water
12 slices toast

Cook the corn in the water until tender. Then remove half the corn and the cooking water to a blender; blend briefly to make a lumpy sauce. Combine the sauce with the other half of the cooked corn and spoon over toast. Using 2 slices per person, there's enough creamed corn here to serve 6. ▪

90. ▪ **Applesauce on raisin bread** is a wonderful combination of sweet fruits.

91. ▪ **Toast can be French without being fat:** Use a nonstick pan and substitute egg whites for half the yolks *(inter.)*. Or eliminate *les oeufs* altogether and use *les bananes* in this recipe from Jennifer Raymond:

▪ BANANA FRENCH TOAST ▪

1 cup chopped ripe banana
1 cup low-fat soy or rice milk
2 to 3 tablespoons flour
Vanilla, cinnamon, and nutmeg to taste

Blend banana and milk until *very smooth* (you need to use a blender for this; a food processor won't give you the necessary smoothness). Add other ingredients and blend to mix. Dip bread and "fry" in a nonstick pan until golden. [Use a medium to medium-low heat setting; this can burn quickly.] ▪

OTHER EGG ALTERNATIVES

92. ▪ **This stand-in for eggs has multiple uses:** for French toast, pancakes, waffles, muffins, cookies, and quick breads. It's taken from a recipe that appeared in the *Washington Post* (December 30, 1992):

▪ EGG SUBSTITUTE ▪

1 cup water
1 tablespoon flax seeds (get them at any health food store)

Combine these in a 2-cup measure and microwave them, uncovered, on full power until the seeds begin to dance and the mixture boils. Continue to boil for 2 to 3 minutes until the mixture has been reduced to about $^3/_4$ cup. Scoop it into the food processor and process for about 30 seconds to break up the seeds. Strain. (Leaving a few seeds in won't hurt.) Refrigerate at least 15 minutes before using; it will last covered in the fridge for 2 weeks. One-fourth cup of it will fill in for one whole egg or two egg whites. ■

93. ■ **For every three-egg omelet,** use one whole egg and two egg whites. You can even use egg whites in a soufflé. Don't overdo your consumption of these, however: they're highly concentrated protein and too much protein can stress the kidneys and make it difficult to stay in positive calcium balance. *Inter.*

94. ■ **Egg white-based egg substitutes** are appreciated by many fat-watchers. If you use them, just be sure that you've read the label on your chosen brand. Their cholesterol content varies and a few brands contain hydrogenated oil. *Inter.*

95. ■ **Tofu can be scrambled like eggs** and measures zip on the cholesterol scale, while a hen's egg has a whopping 220 milligrams of the stuff. The easiest way to get surefire results is to use your tofu with a commercial product called Tofu Scrambler from Fantastic Foods. The package recipe says to cook the tofu with 3 tablespoons of butter or oil. Instead I use one of the oil-free sauté bases from chapter 1—vegetable broth, cooking wine, seasoned rice vinegar, or a combination. *Mod.*

■ BONUS TIP: *If you use eggs, know their source. Getting them from a friend in the country who keeps chickens as a hobby instead of a commercial venture is best. Otherwise, look for a farmer whose chickens are free-roaming and who eat natural foods. As a third choice, buy free-range eggs from a natural foods store. You'll be eating healthier eggs from happier chickens.*

BREAKFAST SPECIALTIES

96. ▪ **Fresh fruit** makes a light and lovely breakfast on its own, or as an inviting prelude to heavier foods. Combine fruits for color and texture: layered kiwi and orange rounds, blueberries with sliced banana, raspberries stuffing half a seeded honeydew, or apple wedges circling a bunch of red or green grapes.

▪ BONUS TIP: *If you like the light feeling you get from eating fruit as your first food of the day but a cold grapefruit is not appealing on a winter morning, take the fruit you want for breakfast out of the refrigerator the night before. That way it will be room temperature when you awaken.*

97. ▪ **For pancakes, use a nonstick griddle and a low-fat recipe.** This one is from Lindsay Wagner (yes, bionic women cook with less fat) and Ariane Spade, and appears in their cookbook, *The High Road to Health.* It makes light, fluffy, perfect pancakes. I can count on being "surprised" with them every Mother's Day and birthday morning.

▪ BASIC PANCAKES ▪

$1^1/_2$ cups whole wheat pastry flour
$1/_4$ teaspoon salt
3 teaspoons baking powder
1 tablespoon cold-pressed vegetable oil
$1^3/_4$ cups soy milk

Combine the flour, salt, and baking powder and sift into a mixing bowl. Combine the oil and soy milk and whip for about 1 minute. Pour into the flour mixture and mix until thoroughly combined. Don't worry about lumps. Preheat a lightly oiled griddle or large skillet. When a few drops of water sprinkled on the griddle bead up and roll off, the griddle is ready. Pour $^1/_4$ cup of the batter at a time onto the griddle. Cook at medium-high heat until the pancakes begin to bubble, about 3 minutes, and the bottoms are lightly browned. If the pancakes bubble up before the bottoms have browned, raise the heat slightly. Turn with a spatula and cook until the second side is lightly browned. (Note: The secret to fluffy eggless pancakes is in beating the liquid ingredients until frothy.) ■

98. ■ **Authentic maple syrup doesn't need butter** to make pancakes Sunday special. A budget-pleasing way to get the taste and fragrance of the genuine article is with Knudsen's Pourable Fruit, Fruit'n Maple flavor, found at natural foods markets. It's a mixture of real maple syrup and grape-sweetened fruit syrup.

99. ■ **Or couple your flapjacks with pure fruit syrup.**

100. ■ **Or your favorite nonfat or soy yogurt.**

101. ■ **Or applesauce or stewed apples.**

102. ■ **Waffles are too wonderful to bother with butter,** especially these substantial multigrain waffles from *The McDougall Health-Supporting Cookbook, Vol. 1,* by Mary McDougall:

■ WAFFLES ■

3 cups water
2 cups rolled oats
1 cup barley flour
$^1/_2$ cup whole wheat pastry flour
1 tablespoon unsulfured molasses or malt syrup

Combine all ingredients in a blender and blend until smooth. Let batter "rest" for 15 minutes. Ladle onto preheated waffle iron. (Use about 1 cup of batter for a 4-section waffle.) *Makes 4 large waffles.* Serve under some of the following toppings: fruit puree, bean soups, [fat-free] gravy, vegetable sauce, or a little pure maple syrup. Helpful hints: To keep warm before serving, place cooked waffles in a warm oven on the bare oven rack. Lightly oil the (even nonstick) waffle iron before heating to prevent sticking. These are very hearty, filling waffles. ■

103. ■ **A traditional Japanese breakfast** is familiar to some travelers since cosmopolitan hotels often offer some variation of it to meet the needs of their Japanese guests. Basic components are rice, miso soup (tip 176), spicy nori or other seaweed, steamed or stir-fried vegetables, often with fish or tofu, and tea. (I originally had this unique breakfast while vacationing in Boston. I'm sure it was the first time I'd ever had broccoli before noon, but it was surprisingly satisfying. I ordered it from room service every day and have since sometimes cooked rice and miso soup on cold mornings.)

CEREALS

104. ■ **Cook hot cereals with extra water** so they'll be creamier without adding milk or butter.

105. ■ **If oatmeal is boring morning after morning,** wake it up with fruit. Banana is a classic, but dried fruits (raisins, currants, or chopped dates or figs) add extra sweetness. (You can add the fruit to your bowl of oatmeal, or cook it as the cereal cooks. This is especially good if you're making old-fashioned oats and letting the cereal cook in a Crockpot overnight.) Chopped apples and pears are another nice addition, with or without raisins; they make your oatmeal crunchy.

106. ■ **Or try other hot grain cereals.** I like Cream of Rye from Roman Meal. It has a nice, nutty taste, is organically grown, and cooks in only three minutes.

107. ■ **Or go for a mixed marriage** of oats and rye, or barley and wheat, or a ready-to-heat mixed grain cereal like Quaker Multi-Grain that has all the aforementioned to keep your mouth and your arteries happy.

108. ■ **Most boxed cereals are free from fat or nearly so.** Pour on nonfat milk, a light rice or soy milk, even fruit juice. Cereals made from whole grains like Kellogg's Nutri-Grain provide plenty of fiber.

109. ■ **Some cereals mix well with nonfat or soy yogurt—** Post Grape-Nuts, for example, some of the heartier flaked cereals, or low-fat granola.

110. ■ **Granola can be a fat disaster, but oil-free granola** is available commercially or from your own oven. This recipe is from Sonnet Pierce, a teenage chef-to-be who has done all the cooking for her family since before she could take driver's ed. Her penchant for creating natural foods recipes using minimal oil has also turned her family into shining examples of the benefits of a low-fat diet.

■ SONNET'S OIL-FREE GRANOLA ■

7 cups old-fashioned rolled oats
2 cups wheat flakes
2 tablespoons sunflower seeds
1 tablespoon chopped walnuts
1 teaspoon cinnamon
$1/4$ cup wheat bran
$1/2$ teaspoon ginger
1 cup medium molasses
$1/3$ cup honey
$1/4$ cup raisins
$1/4$ cup other chopped dried fruit (or more raisins)

Preheat oven to 350 degrees. Mix together in a large bowl all ingredients except raisins and dried fruit. Stir well. Spread on nonstick baking sheet *with sides*. Stir often to avoid burning. (This is why the baking sheet has to have sides—nobody needs an oven full of spilled oats.) Bake until lightly browned. Remove from oven. Stir in raisins and dried fruit. Store in airtight containers. ■

(Variations: Wheat flakes may be substituted with rye or barley flakes, or additional oats. The amount of oil-rich nuts and seeds is small enough to keep the total fat content very low; if you want to lower it still further, substitute Grape-Nuts for the sunflower seeds and walnuts, but add them after baking when you put in the raisins.)

111. ■ **Oil-free granola mixed with applesauce** is an original approach to breakfast.

112. ■ **Wheat germ** earned its reputation as the quintessential health food because of its high concentration of vitamin E, B complex, and zinc. Its fat content, however, is 25 percent of calories—more than most cereals. The best way to get the benefits of wheat (or any grain for that matter) is to eat it whole—bran, germ, endosperm, all of it—instead of fragmented parts of it. If you like the nutty flavor of wheat germ, though, simply use it by the spoonful instead of the bowlful. Put it on other cereals, hot or cold, stir it into nonfat or soy yogurt, or sprinkle it on fruit salad.

■ ■ ■

BREAKFAST BEVERAGES

113. ■ **Freshly squeezed juice** is not only a vitamin-packed way to inaugurate breakfast, it sends a quick message to your brain that you've had some nourishment. Once that's established, you can more easily bypass high-fat items and make healthy choices as to the rest of the meal.

114. ■ **Get in the shake or smoothie habit** with colorful combinations like banana-strawberry, pineapple-mango, or nonfat or soy yogurt with matching frozen fruit (such as blueberry yogurt with frozen blueberries). The sweetest smoothies begin with fruit juice; for less sweetness, start the blender with water, skim milk or a nondairy "milk," or nonfat or soy yogurt. Get the cold, creamy thickness that gives these their treat status with fresh or frozen chopped banana and other frozen fruits. Blend until, well, smoothie!

■ BONUS TIP: *Unsweetened berries, melon balls, peaches, and mixed fruit are in the freezer section at the supermarket. These add a lot of convenience to smoothie-making since they require no washing or chopping and they're available every season of the year.*

115. ■ **Cantaloupe cream** is the lightest, most refreshing summer breakfast you can blend—and so simple. Remove the seeds from one fresh, ripe cantaloupe and chop the fruit into your blender. With an ordinary blender, you'll need to add a little water or juice to get the machine going; with a high-powered blender, the cantaloupe will puree to a thick shake with no added liquid. If you like cold shakes as I do, be sure your melon has been refrigerated for several hours. (See tip 339 for giving cantaloupe cream another incarnation.)

116. ■ **"Coffee?"** When asked that question, most people answer affirmatively, especially in the morning. Nondairy creamers (a misnomer: most contain casein, a milk derivative) aren't usually a great alternative to cream because of the hydrogenated or tropical (saturated) oils in them. You can drink your coffee black, although giving up the cream ended my coffee habit altogether, and I'm probably the better for it. Confirmed coffee drinkers might consider:

117. ▪ **Evaporated skim milk** (it's creamy because it has less water, not more fat).

118. ▪ **Or nonfat dry milk, reconstituted double-strength.**

119. ▪ **Or Westbrae Lite Non Dairy Creamer,** available at health food stores. It is certainly not fat free, but this soy-based product has only 50 percent of the fat in half and half with all the creaminess. (And you can carry your creamer of choice with you in Midgets, shot-size plastic cups with airtight lids from Tupperware.) *Mod.*

120. ▪ **If cappuccino sounds romantic,** the cafe can probably do it for you with skim milk. I know a coffee-drinking vegetarian who brings her own soy creamer to her favorite espresso bar and has cappuccino before work every morning. She says she'll give up caffeine one day, when they start making cappuccino out of Postum.

CHAPTER 3

Get the Fat Out of Salads, Dressings, and Dips

The average man gets most of his fat from meat, the average woman from salad dressing. Eating "just a salad" for lunch every day can be a one-way ticket to Fat City if you're using the typical oily dressings we usually toss with our greens. This is no reason to avoid salad, though. Raw vegetables are nutritional powerhouses bursting with vitamins, minerals, and enzymes. Getting into a salad-a-day pattern—or a two-salads-a-day pattern—is health insurance that pays tangible dividends.

The trick is to dress those salads becomingly. We don't buy clothes that make us look fat, so we shouldn't dress our salads in ways that make them fatty either. There are dozens of hints on the pages that follow for setting off salads with little or no oil and making dips for crudités that aren't based on high-fat sour cream.

For any raw-vegetable dish to be appetizing, start with the freshest, crunchiest vegetables you can get your hands on. I urge you to seek out organically grown produce. In addition to the health and environmental reasons for choosing organic whenever possible, *fresh* organically grown vegetables taste like something you really want to eat—*au naturel* or with a dressing. One of my favorite chefs, Richard Sanell of the Metropolis

American Grill in Kansas City, is adamant about the superiority of organic: "The flavor is so much more intense when the vegetables are organic," he says. "Especially if you get them fresh and locally grown, you take one bite and notice the difference."

And choose vegetables you honestly like. An attitude of "Eat your vegetables, they're good for you" may get some salad into your body, but it will do you a lot more good if you enjoy putting it there.

SALAD DAYS

121. ▪ **Blame boring salads on boring vegetables,** and avoid them with exotics like fennel, kohlrabi, daikon radish, jicama, cilantro, arugula, radicchio, baby corn, amazing mushrooms—Portobello, oyster, enoki—and unusual peppers—Anaheim, banana, and sweet yellow bells.

122. ▪ **Base your salad on a luscious lettuce.** The popularity of oily dressings may have grown from our insistence on eating so much iceberg lettuce. With hearty romaine, tender green and red leaf, sweet Boston and Bibb, tangy endive, and those splendid mixtures of "baby greens," dressing plays a lesser role. (Spinach salad is delicious, too, and it doesn't need bacon or hard-boiled egg crumbled on it.)

123. ▪ **Be sure you even *have* salad** by washing and spin-drying greens when you bring them home and storing them in airtight containers or zipper bags. Washed lettuce is tempting; dirty lettuce wilts in the fridge.

124. ▪ **Beware of bacon bits, cheese chunks, croutons,** olives, and sunflower seeds. They're just fat masquerading as salad.

125. ▪ **Croutons crunch because they're fried** in butter or oil. Instead do a crouton substitute. Mix 2 cups of whole wheat bread crumbs with 1 tablespoon of natural soy sauce and 1 teaspoon of garlic powder. Bake on a cookie sheet at 350 degrees until brown, stirring occasionally. (See also tip 187 in chapter 4.)

126. ▪ **Bread crumbs and bran can top a Caesar salad** as well as nuts or cheese, without adding fat. And nutritional yeast flakes can provide the cheesy flavor. (Note: Nutritional yeast flakes, found at health food stores, are an entirely different product from baker's yeast. Be careful not to confuse the two.)

127. ▪ **Roasted peppers are a delectable salad addition.** To roast red bell peppers, place them on a cookie sheet and broil for about 20 minutes, turning with tongs every 5 minutes or so until the skins are blistered. Then enclose them in a paper bag or a pot with a tight lid and let their own juices steam the peppers for 15 minutes. Take them out of the bag, peel off the skin, remove the seeds, and slice.

128. ▪ **Rub a cut garlic clove on your wooden salad bowl** to impart an unmistakable but never overpowering touch of garlic to an undressed or minimally dressed tossed salad.

129. ▪ **Fresh sprouts are so alive** that they preoccupy taste buds that might otherwise miss an oily dressing. And when any seed is sprouted, its fat content is reduced by approximately two thirds. Try a variety of sprouts to find those you like. I don't care for either of the most popular kinds—alfalfa or mung bean—but I adore sunflower, pea, and peanut sprouts, and I like the red-hot zing that comes from a few mustard, fenugreek, or radish sprouts.

■ BONUS TIP: *Although many natural foods and grocery stores stock an assortment of sprouts, growing your own is easy and gratifying. You can purchase all sorts of sprouting devices, but an easier way to be a kitchen gardener is to:*

(1) Get some quart jars, cheesecloth, and sproutable seeds. Any whole seed or bean will sprout, although some of the larger beans like garbanzos and soy beans are difficult. (If you have garbanzo or soy bean sprouts that you've either grown yourself or purchased at an Asian market, they must be cooked; all the others can be eaten raw.)

(2) Soak the seeds or beans overnight in pure water. Use only 1 or 2 tablespoons per jar of little seeds like alfalfa, up to $^1/_3$ cup for something larger like lentils or mung beans.

(3) Fasten the cheesecloth to the jars with rubber bands and drain off the soaking water.

(4) Rinse and drain the growing sprouts twice a day; prop the jars on their sides in a dish drainer to facilitate drainage.

(5) When sprouts are the length you want them, place in a sunny window for a few hours for chlorophyll to develop in the tiny leaves.

To learn more, see The Sprout Garden: The Indoor Grower's Guide to Gourmet Sprouts *by Mark M. Braunstein.*

130. ■ **Potato salad needn't depend on mayo.** Instead make this picnic favorite that serves two by steaming 10 quartered new potatoes, chopping 3 stalks of celery, and tossing with 2 tablespoons of mustard, and a small jar of capers. (This recipe comes from my literary agent who is not only literary but trim and full of energy for hiking in the California mountains.)

131. ■ **And capers, now that we've mentioned them,** have enough juiciness and bite to make dressing on a green salad redundant. Use half a jar on a salad for two. (Yes, it's an extravagance, but anything you can do to cut fat is cheap compared to bypass surgery.)

132. ▪ **Other tidbits that add interest** to a salad devoid of oily dressings are fresh or pickled ginger, green peppercorns, tiny cocktail onions, those cute little ears of baby corn, and ice-cold gherkins.

133. ▪ **The Germans do a cabbage salad** with a wonderful sweet and sour flavor and no oil. Grate a small head of green cabbage and blend with $1/2$ cup of sugar and $1/2$ to 1 teaspoon of celery seed. Knead the sugar into the cabbage until you have a wet mixture. Then add light vinegar until you achieve the degree of sourness you like. This keeps well refrigerated and tastes best cold.

134. ▪ **The Middle Eastern salad tabouli** is a substantial dish comprised of soaked bulgur (cracked wheat), parsley, mint, tomatoes, optional cucumber, and lemon juice. It is usually in an oil-based marinade, but you can leave the oil out of any tabouli recipe. Simply double the amount of tomatoes (and cucumber if you're using it) and up the lemon juice slightly. Eating tabouli in lettuce leaf wrappers also adds to the moistness of the salad. (You can make tabouli from scratch or from an instant mix. I have successfully used Casbah Tabouli Salad Mix from Sahara Natural Foods and Fantastic Foods Tabouli Salad Mix.)

135. ▪ **To make any salad more substantial,** toss in pasta (colored curls or whole wheat elbows), steamed vegetables (carrots, broccoli, new potatoes), or legumes. Chick-peas (also called garbanzos), kidney beans, and lentils all do well in salad. If you use lentils, stick with brown ones that will stay crisp and hold their shape; save red lentils for soup.

136. ▪ **This salad on skewers,** undoubtedly the prettiest vegetable medley I've ever seen, was served at Dr. Douglas Graham's Club Hygiene in Marathon, Florida. It was developed by Tim Trader, N.D., and Kathy Miller:

■ SALAD KEBABS WITH BARBECUE SAUCE ■

Romaine lettuce leaves
Broccoli and cauliflower florets
Cucumber and zucchini rounds
Cherry tomatoes
Red, yellow, and green bell pepper slices

Barbecue Sauce

$1^{1}/_{2}$ fresh tomatoes
2 large handfuls sun-dried tomatoes (dry—neither soaked
    nor oil-packed)
1 red bell pepper, cored and seeded
1 yellow bell pepper, cored and seeded
2 stalks celery
3 or 4 leaves fresh oregano

Arrange the romaine on individual serving plates. Alternate
the other vegetables on skewers, then place them on the romaine
leaves.

To make Barbecue Sauce: Start a blender with the fresh
and dried tomatoes. Then blend in the bell peppers, celery,
and oregano.

Pour a stripe of sauce on every kebab. Provide extra sauce on
the side. This is a colorful summer meal on its own, or an appropriate red and green first course for a holiday season supper. ■

137. ■ **A fruit is a fruit and a veg is a veg,** but the twain
can meet when you toss sweet raisins or currants into a bowl of
leafy greens, or add apple chunks or orange segments to an otherwise all-vegetable salad.

138. ■ **Expand your definition of crudités** beyond celery,
carrots, peppers, and mushrooms to include cauliflower, fresh

green beans, thinly sliced turnips, broccoli, asparagus, and pea pods. (Any of these can be steamed a bit and chilled before going on the tray.)

DRESSED FOR SUCCESS

139. ■ **Put oil in a spray bottle** and give a salad a squirt to help the seasonings stick to the greens. This is the primary reason oil is used on salads, and it takes only an instant's spray—not a cup or even a tablespoon of oil—to accomplish. *Mod.*

140. ■ **Some salads come already dressed** in a way that adds no fat because of the succulent juiciness of their own ingredients. For example, using a lot of ripe tomatoes, oozing with juice, cuts down on the need for dressing. Or try this from *Fast and Low: Easy Recipes for Low Fat Cuisine,* by Joan Stillman: "One salad made without greens is composed of oranges and red onions, sliced together in the food processor, with its own dressing built in. (For two people, use 2 oranges and $^1/_2$ red onion.)"

141. ■ **Salsa makes a terrific salad dressing.** It can also be served with crudités.

142. ■ **If you didn't like "diet dressing"** ten years ago, take heart in the fact that things are different now. Low-fat and fat-free bottled dressings can be dead ringers for the high-fat dressings they sub for. A lot of people have told me how much they like the Kraft Free dressings, with Peppercorn Ranch and Honey Dijon the particular favorites.

143. ■ **Seasoned rice vinegar** is almost magical in that you can use it all by itself to give your tossed salads a richness that seems oily, even though it is fat free and contains virtually no calories. It's also mild and tastes less acidic than some other vinegars. If you don't find seasoned rice vinegar in the obvious place at the supermarket, look in the aisle where they keep the Oriental foods. (The brand I'm able to get most consistently is Nakano.)

144. ▪ **Other gourmet vinegars that would taste too strong alone** work well when combined with other ingredients. Using vinegars with some genuine taste of their own allows you to use less oil. Try sherry wine, balsamic, and raspberry vinegars.

▪ BONUS TIP: *If you grow herbs in your garden or your kitchen, make your own flavored vinegar with tarragon or other tasty herbs. If you use attractive bottles, these make lovely gifts.*

145. ▪ **Citrus juices can provide the acid tang for oil-free dressings.** Using plain lemon or lime juice on salad isn't some spartan discipline when you have tasty baby greens and don't want to diminish one bit of their subtle flavor with a powerful dressing. Grapefruit works, too. My friend Mary was camping in Ontario with her family when low provisions caused her to improvise a dressing that turned out so well even her kids asked for seconds on salad.

▪ **MARY'S CANADIAN CAMPOUT DRESSING** ▪

$^1/_3$ cup pink grapefruit juice
$^1/_4$ teaspoon salt
$^1/_8$ teaspoon cayenne
A turn of freshly ground black pepper
A few *drops* of canola oil

Place all ingredients in a jar and shake well (or use a blender if you're not camping). If you want a sweeter dressing, add a touch of honey. (Using *fresh* juice makes all the difference in the world, and a little $1.99 citrus juicer is all it takes to get it.) ▪

146. ▪ **Juice can also fill in for half the oil** in a conventional salad dressing recipe. Kathryn Arnold reported in *Delicious!* magazine that using ¼ cup of apple, orange, grapefruit, lemon, or tomato juice with ¼ cup of oil, instead of the ½ cup of oil many recipes call for, can save a whopping 56 grams of fat. *Mod.*

147. ▪ **A dressing of Dijon mustard with fresh lemon juice** and enough vegetable broth to tone down their pungency is simplicity itself. (From Virginia Messina, M.P.H., R.D.)

148. ▪ **Mustard can also replace mayonnaise** fully or in part in many salad dressings. It's lower in fat than mayo and because of its assertive taste, you use less. Mild salad mustard—the kind that's taxi-cab yellow and doesn't cost much—works fine for this. Try it for tuna salad or a vegetarian version that substitutes coarsely mashed chick-peas for tuna in a standard recipe. *Mod.*

149. ▪ **Nonfat or soy yogurt, nonfat buttermilk, or nonfat or soy sour cream** can fill in for regular sour cream or mayonnaise in a dressing recipe.

150. ▪ **Commercial nonfat sour cream makes a good dressing** when combined with garlic, mustard, and lemon juice. You can do the same with soy sour cream. (You can also make your own fat-reduced sour cream substitute from tofu; see tip 267.)

151. ▪ **Perk up commercial nonfat mayonnaise** with a little high-quality, plain, nonfat, or soy yogurt.

152. ▪ **Nonfat buttermilk can be the base for any creamy dressing.** Regular buttermilk has half the fat of whole milk, and low-fat buttermilk cuts this further with no appreciable difference in taste. Tofu and soy yogurt are nondairy options for making dressings creamy.

153. ▪ **Transform vinaigrette into something smooth and creamy** by adding nonfat yogurt, nonfat cottage cheese, or tofu (fat-reduced tofu with $1/3$ less fat than regular works well for this).

154. ▪ **This Dressing for Healthy Coleslaw** comes from *Cooking Without Fat,* by George Mateljan of Health Valley Foods: Mix $1/3$ cup of plain nonfat yogurt, 1 tablespoon of apple cider vinegar, and 2 tablespoons of honey. Toss with your shredded cabbage and *voilà!* You're ready for the potluck.

155. ▪ **Make a marinade based on flavor instead of oil.** This one appeared in *Vegetarian Times* and is used with the permission of its creator, Mary Carroll, coauthor of *The No-Cholesterol (No Kidding!) Cookbook.*

▪ ITALIAN MARINADE ▪

1 teaspoon Dijon mustard
1 tablespoon minced fresh garlic
1 tablespoon minced red onion
$1/4$ cup raspberry vinegar
$1/4$ cup water
1 teaspoon lemon juice
1 teaspoon minced fresh parsley

Whisk together all ingredients in a small bowl. Makes approximately $1/2$ cup. Pour on sliced fresh tomatoes and mushrooms. Top with shredded fresh basil leaves. ▪

156. ▪ **Exotic sesame tahini** may be used in salad dressings if you would prefer an unrefined product to extracted oil. Its fat content is very high, however, so you may wish to cut it half and half with water. *Mod.*

157. ▪ **Ground nuts also provide oiliness** in a dressing without bottled oil. I usually go with raw cashews for this. Toss in $1/4$ cup or so of cashews with a couple of big, juicy tomatoes, a little lemon or lime juice, and seasonings you're fond of (try garlic, basil, ground pepper, sea salt, Mrs. Dash). *Mod.*

■ BONUS TIP: *To save money, buy raw cashew pieces instead of whole raw cashews when you go to the health food store. Since nuts are not used frequently in low-fat cuisine, they should be stored in your freezer so they'll last indefinitely.*

158. ■ **Replace the oil in your recipe with water** and thicken with cornstarch, arrowroot, or kudzu (an Asian starch popular in macrobiotic cuisine). To use these thickeners, mix about 2 tablespoons plus 2 teaspoons of one of them with 1 cup of cold water. Heat to just below the boiling point while beating with an eggbeater. Chill and mix with other dressing ingredients. (I used to leave the amounts to kitchen intuition when I used this technique; thanks go to Elaine French for educating me on the proper proportions.)

159. ■ **Vegetable broth** can also be used to supplant the oil. If you want a thicker dressing, blend in a little cornstarch.

160. ■ **Leftover pasta** is not only good stir-fried with vegetables but it can be used instead of oil in a salad dressing recipe. Blend the pasta with water and/or the other wet ingredients the original recipe calls for and use the resultant thick slurry to replace the oil. The replacement amounts are not exact: Start with a little pasta and puree it with the other dressing ingredients until the proper consistency is reached, adding more pasta as needed. (They've been doing this to cut the fat in dressings at Milly's in San Rafael for several years.)

161. ■ **Vegetables can make the dressing** as well as take the dressing, as in this one contributed by Susan Smith Jones, Ph.D., author of *Choose to Be Healthy, Choose to Live Peacefully,* and *Choose to Live Each Day Fully.* In her honor, I've called it:

■ ■ ■

CHOOSE TO BE
▪ FAT-FREE SALAD DRESSING ▪

1 large garden tomato, quartered
Juice of $^1/_2$ lemon
1 tablespoon balsamic vinegar
Herbs of your choice
Bragg's Liquid Aminos to taste

Blend and serve with greens. (As for choosing those herbs, fresh basil and oregano are naturals with tomato. And Bragg's Liquid Aminos are an unfermented substitute for tamari soy sauce, which could also be used in this recipe.) For a creamy French style dressing, 2 tablespoons of sesame tahini (*mod.*) can be added. ▪

162. ▪ **Or improvise your own very-veggie dressing** by starting your blender with quartered tomatoes, tomato juice or V-8, and adding fresh lemon or lime juice, your choice of vinegar, and other seasonings (such as onion, garlic, shallot, basil, ginger, tarragon). Add raw vegetables—cucumber, sweet pepper, baby carrots—for body until the desired thickness is reached.

163. ▪ **Befriend a fat-conscious chef** and get his or her favorite dressing recipe, or borrow this one from chef Michael Forsberg of Cafe Balabans in St. Louis:

▪ LIME YOGURT VINAIGRETTE ▪

2 tablespoons fresh lime juice
$^1/_2$ tablespoon red wine vinegar
1 small garlic clove, minced
1 teaspoon Dijon mustard
6 tablespoons plain, nonfat yogurt
$^1/_4$ teaspoon salt
Pinch finely ground black pepper

In a small bowl, mix lime juice, vinegar, garlic, and mustard. Whisk in yogurt. Add salt and pepper. This can be made 2 hours ahead of time and stored in the refrigerator. ■

Variations: (1) Substitute lemon juice for lime juice. (2) Increase the Dijon mustard to 2 teaspoons for use on spinach salad. (3) Roast cumin seeds in a dry, heavy cast iron skillet on low heat. When they're ready, you'll start to smell a luscious cumin scent in your kitchen. Let them cool and grind in a coffee grinder or with a mortar and pestle; add $1/4$ teaspoon to the dressing for an Indian twist.

TAKE A DIP

164. ■ **A quick dip** using the dried herbs you have on hand comes from my mother, Gladys Marshall. (People drop in at her house and she always feeds them. Moms are like that.)

■ SPICE SHELF VEGGIE DIP ■

1 cup low-fat cottage cheese
$1/2$ teaspoon each onion powder, garlic powder, dried basil
1 teaspoon dried minced chives
2 teaspoons parsley flakes
1 tablespoon lemon juice

Blend cottage cheese until smooth. Gently mix in seasonings and lemon juice; let sit in the fridge. (Note: You can make this with nonfat instead of low-fat cottage cheese, but you'll need to add a touch of nonfat milk or yogurt to provide sufficient moisture. You can also create a similar dip using tofu—silken tofu works best—and adding to the ingredients $1/2$ to 1 teaspoon salt to taste.)

■ BONUS TIP: *Tofu comes in a variety of consistencies. Extra-firm and firm are best for cooked dishes that call for the tofu to be used in slices or chunks. Soft or silken tofu is ideal for dips, spreads, or any recipe that requires putting the tofu in a blender or food processor. It gets confusing when a package says "silken firm" or some other contradictory phrase, but I keep it straight by remembering that silken is always on the soft side, in spite of paradoxical labeling.*

165. ■ **Plain nonfat or soy yogurt makes a dandy dip.**

166. ■ **And even a virtually fatless "guacamole" is possible** if you use peas instead of avocado for the base. This recipe comes from chef Mark Hall and appears in *Dr. Dean Ornish's Program for Reversing Heart Disease:*

■ **GREEN PEA "GUACAMOLE"** ■

3 cups green peas, fresh or frozen
2 tablespoons lemon juice
1 cup chopped red onion
2 teaspoons finely minced garlic
1 teaspoon ground cumin
$1/4$ teaspoon freshly ground black pepper
$1/8$ teaspoon cayenne
Salt

If using fresh peas, steam them, retaining their bright green color. Do not overcook. If using frozen peas, just defrost them. Puree the peas in a blender or food processor with the lemon juice, onion, garlic, cumin, and black pepper. Add the cayenne and salt to taste. ■

167. ■ **Avocado guacamole can be made lower in fat** by stretching the avocado with broccoli. This recipe comes from

Sue Douglas and was printed in *Health Science,* the membership journal of the American Natural Hygiene Society (*mod.*):

■ BROCCOMOLE ■

1 pound raw broccoli
6 tablespoons sweet red pepper
1 large avocado
4 tablespoons lemon juice
4 tablespoons dried chives (optional)

Peel stems of broccoli. Cut stems and florets into even-size pieces, lightly steam, and allow to cool. Dice sweet red pepper. Remove skin and seed from avocado and scoop out the flesh. Place all ingredients in a blender. Puree until mixed, but showing the distinct color of the peppers. This is a very tasty dip or dressing for your salad. ■

168. ■ **A fiery dip** (not for the faint of heart or palate) can be made by adding a touch of harissa, a hot, hot condiment found in Middle Eastern markets, to a creamy base like tofu (salted or marinated) or nonfat cottage cheese. Longtime gourmet cook Mildred Aissen makes this with cottage cheese and a bit of anchovy paste. She also adds egg whites and layers it between slices of baked eggplant and low-fat mozzarella for moussaka. *Inter.*

169. ■ **Hummus is a Middle Eastern delicacy** traditionally made with chick-peas, sesame tahini, and olive oil. You can get the texture and much of the taste of hummus by simply blending canned chick-peas (drain them but reserve the liquid; you'll need a little of it to get your blender or processor going). Season them with lemon juice, garlic, mint, a dash of Tabasco, and salt or a little juice from a can of olives. This is good for dipping veggies, spreading on pita, or stuffing scooped-out cherry tomatoes. (You're right: it requires either great patience or mild neurosis to actually scoop out cherry tomatoes, but stuffed with hummus they do make enchanting hors d'oeuvres.)

170. ▪ **A Southwestern alternative to hummus** from Margaret Malone calls for seasoning blended chick-peas with lime juice, oregano, cilantro, and chipotle chiles—the smoked jalapeños you can get at Latin specialty stores and in some of those hot spice shops in the malls.

171. ▪ **This tofu dip is always in my fridge.** It also doubles as mayonnaise in dressings and on sandwiches. Although regular tofu gets nearly half of its calories from the soy oil it contains, it's a pretty decent fat with a good balance of fatty acids. And this dip can fill in for standard mayonnaise that chalks up 90 percent of its calories from fat, plus cholesterol from the eggs it contains. Fat-reduced tofu (much less fat) is also on the market. If you choose to use fat-reduced tofu for this dip, add 1 to 2 tablespoons of water to the recipe. *Mod.*

▪ TOFU DIP ▪

6 ounces soft or medium tofu
2 tablespoons lemon juice
$1/2$ teaspoon salt
$1/4$ teaspoon white pepper
Optional seasonings to taste: onion powder, garlic powder,
    and finely chopped pickle

Puree all ingredients in a blender or food processor fitted with the metal blade until creamy. Adjust seasonings to your liking. Keeps well refrigerated in an airtight container for up to 5 days. ▪

CHAPTER 4

Get the Fat Out of
Soups and Sauces

H ot soup is the ultimate comfort food. It's like a back rub you can eat. Teamed with a thick slice of bread and a crisp salad, soup is a fine lunch, whether you're eating at the kitchen table or your desk at the office. It can also be an appetizing introduction to a heavier meal. Some urbane restaurants routinely serve soup as a first course, and salad after the entree to clear the palate before dessert.

Regardless of when you eat it, soup can add unnecessarily to your daily fat allotment or fit well within it. It all depends on what goes into the soup pot. Is the soup based on fatty meats or cream, or on beans or vegetables that have almost no fat? Is the liquid in it high-fat beef or chicken stock, or a fat-reduced or fat-free broth? Do the flavors come from fresh ingredients and carefully chosen seasonings, or is there a sheet of oil floating on top that adds far more greasiness than savor?

The same questions can be asked about gravies and sauces. Although they can turn a so-so dish into something special, they can also turn its fat content into something scandalous. But the added taste and texture we expect from sauces needn't depend on fats or oils; in fact, too much of these can diminish those very qualities. Although there is much to be said for good, plain food, we don't have to do without the luxury of toppings. We simply have to be willing to alter our old ideas as to what constitutes a sauce and cook accordingly.

Read the sections covering both soups and sauces, even if you're interested in only one or the other. Many of the same techniques apply to both. Today's soup can become tomorrow's sauce, and today's gravy can admirably thicken tomorrow's chowder.

TAKING STOCK

172. ■ **The easiest way to get a light vegetable broth** is to simply save the water over which you've steamed vegetables. If you want more intensity, boil some vegetables or vegetable trimmings in the broth. (If you're using cabbage family members, turn down the heat just before the broth reaches the boiling point; otherwise it will release an unpleasant ultra-cabbage smell.) Freeze the broth in ice-cube trays so you'll always have some on hand.

173. ■ **Or use a broth powder.** I like several from the health food store including Bernard Jensen's Broth or Seasoning from Hidden Valley Mills and Vogue Instant Vege Base.

174. ■ **Or follow a recipe.** This one comes from the classic meatless cookbook *Ten Talents,* by Rosalie Hurd and Dr. Frank Hurd:

■ VEGETABLE BROTH ■

2 cups sliced potatoes with skins
2 cups thinly sliced carrots

2 cups thinly sliced turnips
2 cups green pea pods
1 onion, sliced
Outer leaves of lettuce
Outer leaves of cabbage
Odd stalks of asparagus
Salt to taste
Parsley, for garnish

Wash all the vegetables, discarding the wilted parts. Slice and put them into a large saucepan. Cover with water. Bring to a boil, and let simmer for 2 hours. Then strain. Add salt to taste. Garnish with chopped fresh parsley. ■

175. ■ **Equal parts tomato juice or V-8 and water** make a no-work base for minestrone.

176. ■ **Miso, a savory Japanese soy product,** makes a lovely soup broth. There are several varieties of miso; I prefer white miso for its delicate nature. Traditional miso soup uses only sautéed onions and carrots with the optional addition of mushrooms and noodles in a miso broth. It's a superb soup when you're feeling feverish or stuffy in the nose. (A neighbor brought me miso soup with a touch of brandy in it when I had a cold last year. I felt better afterward, although I couldn't be sure whether to thank the miso or the brandy.)

Miso broth is a welcome addition to any soup. Cook your basic ingredients in water and at the end of cooking bring the water down to a gentle simmer. Ladle out a little of the hot broth into a cup. Mix miso into it (start with 4 to 5 tablespoons of miso for every quart of liquid in the soup) to make a liquid paste. Return the miso paste you've made to the soup pot to allow its mellow flavor to permeate the broth. Take care not to let the miso boil. (You can find miso in Oriental markets, natural foods stores, and many supermarkets. Also look for it in a convenient instant powdered form called Miso-Cup from Edward & Sons.)

177. ▪ **Bean soups don't need to start with stock** since bean broth is so flavorful already.

178. ▪ **Many soups can do without a premade soup base** by using trimmings from the vegetables you'll use in the soup to make a stock on the spot. According to *Dr. Dean Ornish's Program for Reversing Heart Disease,* "If you are making a leek, potato, and mushroom soup, take the roots and greens of the leeks, the potato peelings and maybe even an extra potato, and the mushroom ends. Cover them with 5 or 6 cups cold water, add a bay leaf, some parsley branches, and a pinch of thyme, bring to a boil, then simmer for 20 minutes or longer, if you have the time. Or with an asparagus-pea soup, use the ends of the asparagus, the pea pods, some parsley, bay leaves, and maybe a few onion slices, and make a quick stock."

179. ▪ **If you choose to use chicken broth** (*inter.*), you can greatly reduce its fat content by letting the stock sit in the refrigerator overnight and skimming off the surface fat before making your soup. There are also some defatted, canned chicken broths available at both health food and grocery stores. Chicken-flavored broth powders containing no chicken are another option, as is substituting vegetable broth.

SOUP BASICS

180. ▪ **Soup recipes are always open to alteration,** and that includes exchanging high-fat ingredients for low-fat ones. When you make soup, you can play more freely with ingredients, seasonings, and length of simmering time than in any other kind of cooking. Unless it's overly salted or the rice or potatoes are underdone, you can't make many serious mistakes with soup.

■ BONUS TIP: *Long cooking over low heat makes soup especially thick and rich-tasting.*

181. ■ **Satisfying soup combines vegetables with a starch or protein.** Therefore, soup takes naturally to recycled leftovers. Rice reheats quickly in soup, as do beans and noodles. And last night's baked potatoes can be peeled, diced, and tossed in at the end of cooking soup to just heat them through.

182. ■ **Black bean soup** is one of my favorites because it can change character dramatically with the addition of different seasonings: balsamic vinegar, sherry, cayenne or spicy harissa, even a bit of brown sugar.

183. ■ **Tamarind soup is an imported treat** found in Asian groceries in paste form or dehydrated in packets like the instant soup we're more familiar with. Introduced to me by Mildred Aissen, tamarind soup imparts an intriguing sourness to any hot or cold soup made of pureed greens. It also makes a hearty winter soup with cubed or dehydrated potatoes, or a cold soup for summer with salad greens, chopped scallions and cucumber, and a dollop of plain, nonfat yogurt.

For Chinese hot and sour soup, use a packet of tamarind soup instead of the usual seasonings. Add white pepper—very important for the characteristic taste—and the tiniest bit of *(mod.)* sesame oil.

184. ■ **If you're making a soup with meat** *(inter.)*, cut the amount by half and use more vegetables. Prepare your soup a day ahead and keep it in the fridge overnight so the fat will thicken at the top to be skimmed off easily. (See tip 218.)

185. ■ **Seitan replaces meat beautifully in soups.** Seitan is wheat gluten you can buy ready-made or make yourself, either from flour (quite a job) or from a boxed mix like Arrowhead Mills Seitan Quick Mix. There is only 1 gram of fat and no cholesterol in a 2¹/₂-ounce serving, about what you'd get in a substantial bowl of soup. Seitan has a very meaty texture but a fairly bland flavor. For it to be as delicious as it can be in a soup, let it spend some time cooking in seasoned broth to inherit some of the tang that surrounds it. (For more on seitan, see tip 286.)

186. ▪ **My favorite onion soup contains no oil,** no beef stock, no melted cheese, but it's as warming and welcome when I'm under the weather as chicken noodle ever was. This is the creation of Mary McDougall and appears in *The McDougall Plan:*

▪ ONION SOUP ▪

3 onions, chopped or sliced
¹/₄ cup water
4 cups vegetable stock or water
2 tablespoons sodium-reduced tamari [soy sauce]
¹/₂ teaspoon dry mustard [optional]
Dash of thyme [optional]
¹/₄ teaspoon garlic powder [optional]

Sauté onions in the ¹/₄ cup water. Cook for about 15 minutes, until soft and tender. Add the 4 cups vegetable stock or water and bring to a boil. Reduce heat to low. Add the tamari [and optional seasonings]. Simmer covered for at least 30 minutes before serving. The longer it cooks, the more flavor it will have. ▪

187. ▪ **Garnish your soup with fat-free croutons** instead of using fried ones. To make these, cut crustless bread slices in ¹/₂-inch squares and broil them briefly until browned, first on one side, then the other. (Keep a watchful eye; croutons can char quickly.) If you want your croutons seasoned, toss with a little tamari and some nutritional yeast flakes or (*mod.*) a tiny amount of grated dairy or soy Parmesan cheese.

188. ■ **Ramen noodles** with their yummy Far Eastern flavor make an almost instant lunch-in-a-bowl soup. Most, however, are fried, so look for a brand like Westbrae that uses baked noodles. The fat savings is some 80 percent.

189. ■ **For the taste of ham** in bean or split pea soup, season with sage to provide the "phantom flavor" of ham or add a few of the best meatless bacon-flavored bits you can find. (My preference is for Fakin' Bacon Bits by Lightlife Foods.) There is also a product at some health food stores called Bakon Yeast—smoked, dried torula yeast—that gives a distinctive ambience of hickory smoke to bean soups and baked beans.

190. ■ **A bit of tofu pureed with water in a blender** (*mod.*) can thicken soup. Remove cooked soup from the heat source and add the tofu/water puree (after the soup has cooled for a minute or two to keep the tofu from curdling). An alternative is to add the tofu/water puree to cold soup and heat to just below the boiling point. Other dependable thickeners that don't add fat include:

191. ■ **Farina, flour, or cornstarch** (dissolve 1 tablespoon of the powder in 2 tablespoons of water to make the paste you'll stir into the soup).

192. ■ **A couple of ladles of the soup you're making** taken from the pot, pureed in the blender, then added back to the soup for a more substantial broth.

193. ■ **Or potatoes, which can provide thickness in almost any soup.** When it's creaminess in a blended soup that you're after, put 1 or 2 diced potatoes in the pot with the other ingredients. When you put the soup in the blender to puree, the potatoes will guarantee that your soup is cream-of-what-have-you.

To thicken a noncream soup, just dice raw, peeled potatoes (approximately 1 potato for every 3 cups of soup) in enough water to cover, and cook until tender. Then blend the potatoes in your blender with the cooking liquid only, and add this to your soup as it cooks.

194. ■ **Other starchy vegetables also thicken cream soup** or even make a cream soup by themselves. I often cook frozen peas in vegetable stock or water seasoned with broth powder, dried herbs, and a little ground sea salt, and blend the whole thing in the blender. The result is a soft green, creamy soup in nothing flat.

SOUP'S OTHER HATS

195. ■ **When something you're cooking calls for sautéing,** use thin soup or soup broth instead of oil.

196. ■ **A hearty soup can top a baked potato** instead of butter or sour cream. (There are many more suggestions for ways to dress up a potato in chapter 5.)

197. ■ **Turn soup into stew** by cooking it longer and letting it get really thick, or by using it for soup the first day and reheating the thickened leftovers the next.

198. ■ **Some soups can even become sandwich spreads** when they've been refrigerated overnight and thereby thicken to a spread consistency. This works especially well with split pea soup. Spread cold leftover split pea soup on hot toast and it almost seems to melt; enhance with Dijon mustard, leaf lettuce, and a slice of beefsteak tomato.

199. ■ **Dip thick chunks of bread in your soup** (it's okay—

the manners patrol isn't watching). This makes such a satisfying meal, and the soup-dunked bread never asks for butter.

200. ▪ **With all these uses, make a large batch of soup** on the weekend and have it on hand for quick meals throughout the week.

A SAUCE FOR ALL SEASONS

201. ▪ **Use vegetable puree as a sauce** instead of one based on butter. Simply puree the veggies in their cooking water with a pinch of salt and your choice of seasonings.

202. ▪ **Chutney is a clever topping for grains,** I was reminded by Nava Atlas, author of *American Harvest.* Suit your taste, sweet or hot.

203. ▪ **This ersatz cheese sauce**—genuinely fat free— comes from Elaine French, who teaches classes on low-fat, natural foods cooking in Honolulu:

▪ VEGGIE-CHEEZ SAUCE ▪

1 cup chopped onions
1 cup diced carrots
2 cups cooked (or canned) white beans
2 cups bean cooking liquid or water
Salt to taste (may not be necessary if using canned beans)
2 garlic cloves (optional)
Crushed red pepper to taste (optional)

Sauté onions and carrots in water until soft. Puree them in a blender with the cooked white beans and the cooking liquid or water and salt. If the garlic or red pepper is appropriate for the dish that will receive the sauce, add one or both of these while blending. ■

204. ■ **When you want a white sauce** to use over vegetables or in any recipe calling for cream sauce, you may want to try this one from *The No Salt, No Sugar, No Fat Cookbook,* by Jacqueline B. Williams with Goldie Silverman:

■ WHITE SAUCE ■

$^1\!/_2$ cup instant nonfat dry milk
1 tablespoon flour
1 tablespoon cornstarch or arrowroot
Pepper to taste
1 cup chicken stock [*inter.*] or vegetable stock

Combine all ingredients except stock in a saucepan. Add stock slowly to avoid lumps. Mix until smooth. Cook, stirring over low heat until sauce thickens. Serve warm over cooked vegetables. Makes 1 cup of sauce. ■

Variations: (1) Sauté 1 cup of sliced mushrooms in $^1\!/_4$ cup of stock and add to sauce. (2) Add 2 or 3 tablespoons chopped chives. (3) Add $^1\!/_2$ teaspoon garlic powder and 1 tablespoon onion powder. (4) Add freshly grated nutmeg to sauce just before serving.

(I have made a nondairy version of the above sauce by substituting soy milk powder for the instant nonfat dry milk. Since soy powder does not dissolve instantly, it needs to be blended with the broth and then put in the saucepan.)

205. ■ **Use the slurry method** to make a pleasingly thick sauce for a stir-fry vegetable or curry dish in its own wok or skillet. Chef Michael Forsberg taught me to make this slurry from 1 to 2 tablespoons of cold water (you can use soy sauce for part of the water) and 1 teaspoon of cornstarch or tapioca flour. The mixture should be thin enough that you can stir it with a chopstick or your finger until the lumps are gone. As you near the end of the cooking process, push aside the food in the wok or skillet and add the slurry to the liquid that's there. If you want more thickness, make another slurry and repeat. If it's too thick, add a bit of plain water. (This technique works with soups, too.)

206. ■ **Good barbecue sauce** is like an alarm clock that wakes up the spirit of grilled onions, veggie burgers, even corn on the cob, minimizing or eliminating the need for oil, mayonnaise, and butter respectively. Read the label and try to get a brand that's oil free.

207. ■ **Cocktail sauce is a better choice than tartar sauce** (it saves 8 grams of fat per tablespoon).

208. ■ **Or you can make this alternative tartar sauce** from *The Pritikin Program for Diet & Exercise,* by Nathan Pritikin and Patrick McGrady, Jr. Add to a fat-reduced mayonnaise: capers, mustard, finely chopped onion, garlic, dill weed, other appropriate herbs of your choice, and an optional dash of lemon juice.

209. ■ **What's an artichoke without butter? Very good** when you dip it section by section in this sauce from *The American Vegetarian Cookbook from the Fit for Life Kitchen,* by Marilyn Diamond:

■ OIL-FREE HERB SAUCE ■

1^1/$_2$ cups vegetable stock
1 sprig fresh thyme, or ^{1}/$_4$ teaspoon dried
1 small piece bay leaf
1 garlic clove
^{1}/$_2$ teaspoon lemon juice

Place stock, thyme, bay leaf, and garlic in a saucepan. Boil to reduce by half. Add lemon juice and pour over vegetables or use as a dip for artichokes. *Yields* ^{3}/$_4$ *cup.* ■

Note: To reheat cold artichokes, place in a baking dish, cover them with this sauce, cover loosely with foil, and bake for 20 minutes at 375 degrees.

PLEASING ON PASTA

210. ▪ **Pasta sauce** can be a surprising source of fat, although there are brands with no added oil that are well worthy of a red-checkered tablecloth and maybe a little *vino*. Sauces I especially like are those from Millina's Finest. The Millina's sauces were created as a tribute to the founder's grandparents, Rafael and Millina Caparone Battendieri. With names that Italian, this has to be great sauce. (As a bonus, the tomatoes, onion, and basil used are all certified organic.)

211. ▪ **Or become a low-fat Italian chef yourself** and concoct an enviable fresh tomato sauce for your pasta. I try to get Italian plum tomatoes and slowly roast them—about 2 hours at 250 degrees until the skins can be eased off with little trouble. I mix the tomatoes in a large, nonstick skillet with minced garlic, chopped onions, zucchini, and eggplant that have been sautéing in red wine, vegetable broth, or tomato juice. I add more wine, broth, or juice to provide enough liquid for a sauce and season with basil (fresh when it's available) and a bit of oregano, plus salt and freshly ground black pepper to taste.

As a thin, chunky sauce, this can be served immediately. For a thicker sauce and thoroughly mingled flavors, simmer over low heat for an hour or an afternoon, checking periodically to be sure there is plenty of liquid in the pan.

▪ BONUS TIP: *Whenever you cook with wine, be sure to allow enough time for the alcohol to cook off and only the rich flavor to remain.*

212. ▪ **Make lentils soupy with extra water** or by adding tomato sauce, season to your liking, and serve on pasta.

213. ▪ **Piquant pesto** is usually eliminated in low-fat diets, but you can play with your pesto recipe and reduce or eliminate the pine nuts and oil in the traditional fresh basil sauce. Mary Carroll, coauthor of *The No Cholesterol (No Kidding!) Cookbook*, has created a scrumptious pesto with only 1 gram of fat per serving. She shared this recipe with readers of her column, "Low-Fat Kitchen," in *Vegetarian Times* magazine:

▪ LOW-FAT PESTO ▪

2 cups chopped fresh basil leaves
1 cup chopped fresh Italian (flat-leaf) parsley
$1/4$ cup toasted bread crumbs
2 tablespoons grated Parmesan cheese
2 garlic cloves, minced
3 tablespoons light miso
$1/4$ to $1/3$ cup water

In a food processor, combine basil, parsley, bread crumbs, Parmesan, garlic, and miso; pulse until mixture is finely minced. With machine running, add water until pesto is smooth and creamy. *Serves 6.* ▪

214. ▪ **A quarter-cup of cooked beans** can be "blenderized" with a cup of water or tomato juice as a quick sauce for pasta, rice, or cooked veggies. "Spice as you like," says this tip's contributor, Joanne Saltzman, author of *Amazing Grains*. (You can even add a splash of red wine or nonalcoholic beer.)

215. ▪ **Primavera means "in the style of springtime,"** but since the spring veggies are smothered in heavy cream sauce, this kind of springtime can lead to a pudgy summer. Instead, make your primavera sauce in a no-fat base. Sauté garden vegetables, such as fresh or frozen green peas, broccoli and cauliflower florets, chopped baby carrots, and red bell pepper, in a combination of flavorful vegetable broth, dry white wine, and minced garlic and red onion. Add sea salt, ground pepper, rosemary, and more broth or wine for simmering. (You can spoon the primavera sauce over any pasta, but I prefer tossing it with multicolored spiral noodles and serving this palette of springtime as a one-dish meal.)

216. ▪ **Peanut sauce** gives the quintessential Thai touch to cold or hot noodles, rice, vegetables, or the meaty Indonesian soy patty, tempeh. Based on peanut butter, peanut sauce is never going to be fat free. Nevertheless, this one from seventeen-year-old aspiring chef Sonnet Pierce is light on fat but heavy on exotic style (*mod.*):

▪ THAILANDISH PEANUT SAUCE ▪

1 tablespoon orange juice concentrate
$1/2$ cup water
2 chopped scallions
1 tablespoon minced green pepper
1 tablespoon minced fresh ginger
$1/4$ cup smooth natural peanut butter
Juice of 1 lemon
2 teaspoons tamari soy sauce
1 tablespoon rice wine or water

Heat the orange juice concentrate with $1/4$ cup of the water. In the orange juice concentrate mixture, sauté the scallions, green pepper, and ginger until the pepper is tender and the white bulbs of the scallions are translucent. Whisk the remaining ingredients together in a small bowl; add to the sautéed mixture. Heat over low heat, stirring constantly until warmed through. Add additional soy sauce if desired and extra water if too thick. ▪

(Note: Natural peanut butter is called for because most

commercial peanut butter contains hydrogenated oils. The freshest natural peanut butter is the kind you grind yourself at the store from nothing but roasted peanuts.)

■ BONUS TIP: *If you're convinced of the nutritional importance of dark leafy greens like kale and collards but your children will have none of them, hide them in pasta sauces. Use kitchen shears to cut pieces of raw greens—only the tender leaves, not the tough stems—into a portion of the sauce and blend in the blender to finely chop the greens. In thick tomato sauces, the greens are virtually indistinguishable. By the time my daughter got wise to this trick, she had outgrown her aversion to all things green and leafy.*

THE REST IS GRAVY

217. ■ **Mashed potatoes are at their best with this fat-free brown gravy**—so are other vegetables and grains. It's from *The McDougall Health-Supporting Cookbook, Vol. 1,* by Mary A. McDougall:

■ SIMPLE BROWN GRAVY ■

7 tablespoons whole wheat flour
2 cups cold water
$1/4$ teaspoon onion powder
$1/8$ teaspoon garlic powder
1 teaspoon minced dried onion
1 tablespoon salt-reduced tamari (soy sauce)

In a saucepan, combine flour and water. Stir until well blended and cook over low heat until thickened, about 10 minutes. Add the remaining ingredients. Continue to cook over low heat for 10 minutes, stirring occasionally. ∎

218. ∎ **If you're tending the gravy at your mom's on Thanksgiving** and it's conventional gravy with conventional grease, refrigerate it before serving and discard the solid fat that rises to the top. (I learned about a device specifically for this purpose called the Grease Out, an acrylic pitcher that lets you pour defatted gravy or soup off the bottom after the fat has risen. You can order it from Lehman's Non-Electric Catalog, P.O. Box 41, Kidron, OH 44636.) *Inter.*

219. ∎ **Thicken gravy with pureed beans.**

220. ∎ **Or with cornstarch, kudzu, or arrowroot** instead of flour and fat. As a rule of thumb, 1 tablespoon of these thickeners works where 2 tablespoons of butter did before.

∎ **Or you can leave added fat out of a traditional gravy** by first toasting the flour called for. Use a dry skillet and medium heat; stir the flour until it's just browned. Then mix in the liquid called for with a wire whisk until smooth. Heat over low flame, stirring constantly, until the gravy achieves the thickness you want.

222. ∎ **Specialty flours like garbanzo and barley** (at natural foods stores and Indian markets) make a piquant base for fat-free gravies. Water-sautéed onions and garlic are a welcome addition, too. Here's a recipe to try from *Cooking with Natural Foods,* by Muriel Beltz:

∎ GARBANZO FLOUR GRAVY ∎

$^1/_2$ cup garbanzo flour

2 cups water (water left after cooking potatoes may be used for part of the liquid)

$^1/_2$ teaspoon salt

$^1/_4$ teaspoon onion powder
$^1/_8$ teaspoon garlic powder
$^1/_8$ teaspoon celery seed
1 teaspoon minced onion
3 tablespoons soy sauce
2 teaspoons dried parsley or 2 tablespoons fresh parsley

In a saucepan, blend the garbanzo flour in the water (flour may be browned before blending if desired). Add salt, onion powder, garlic powder, celery seed, minced onion, soy sauce, and parsley. Cook on low heat until thickened. ■

Variation: Other flours can be used in place of garbanzo flour, such as whole wheat, barley, millet, etc. Use less or more seasoning to your taste.

223. ■ **Bean stock** makes a mouth-watering gravy—easy, too, if you save and freeze the liquid every time you cook beans. Simply thaw and mix 4 tablespoons of bean stock (I keep wanting to say, "Jack and the . . .") with 1 tablespoon of flour. Heat slowly and stir constantly to prevent burning. Virginia Messina, M.P.H., R.D., reminded me that some bean stocks—lima, for example—thicken by themselves, so you can have gravy without adding flour. Either way, this is a reasonable alternative to using fatty meat juices.

CHAPTER 5

Get the Fat Out of
Entrees and Side Dishes

When it comes to entrees and side dishes, we have two jobs to do. The first is obvious: to reduce the fat content in the main dishes and accompaniments we eat right now. The second is less blatant but even more important: to let go of the old thinking that gave certain foods entree rank and kept other satisfying foods in the "on the side" category. This is crucial because traditional main dishes in our culture have been those high in cholesterol, total fat, and saturated fat, while the grains, beans, and vegetables that have attended them are cholesterol free, generally low in overall fat, and very low in saturated fat.

My personal trainer (one of those incredible women who doesn't look a day over twenty but swears she's thirty two and has four kids) says that upgrading side dishes to center stage was the first dietary change she made. Erstwhile extras like rice, potatoes, and beans became the answer to "What's for dinner?" and meats took a supporting role, causing the aggregate fat content of her family's diet to plummet.

Anyone can begin this way by having a vegetable stir-fry with a little chicken instead of a chicken stir-fry with a few vegetables; or having a chef's-style salad with some beef chunks instead of a hunk of beef overshadowing a tiny bowl of pale head lettuce.

You will cut saturated fat and total fat even more—while adding fiber and complex carbohydrates to your diet—every time you opt for a grain, bean, or starchy vegetable entree. The time has come for these to take center stage without apology. *Do not underestimate the major, positive changes that can take place in your health when you see the value of promoting starches to entree level and choosing more and more of your foods from the plant kingdom.*

Even the very leanest cuts of beef, with all visible fat trimmed and cooked by the best methods we know of, get no less than 29 percent of calories from fat. And very lean chicken—white meat with the skin removed—gets about 19 percent of its calories from fat. (Like all animal products, both beef and chicken contain cholesterol.) Compare these figures with those of other entree choices—4 percent of calories from fat for kidney beans, 3 percent for spaghetti or sweet potatoes, 1 percent for white potatoes, and no cholesterol in any of them.

Creating entrees from foods like these gives you culinary license within low-fat parameters. "If you base your diet on grains, vegetables, beans, and fruit," Joanne Saltzman, author and founder of the School of Natural Cookery in Boulder, explained to me, "using a little olive oil when it would add to the integrity of the dish is fine. It provides a lot of satisfaction for a little bit of fat."

There are plenty of tips here for using beans, grains, pasta, potatoes, and the cuisines of the world to create exciting main dishes. And remember what we've covered already: a thick soup with warm bread or a big salad with chick-peas or steamed new potatoes can be entrees, too.

Use the intermediate tips as you need them to ease yourself

along, or if you're eager to go all the way with this, skip them altogether. However you proceed, congratulate yourself on the progress you're making—and have a nice dinner.

AMBER WAVES OF GRAINS (AND BEANS)

224. ■ **Rice provides satiety without fat.** This staple food for much of the rest of the world is also a staple in low-fat kitchens here at home. White and brown rice are both virtually devoid of fat, but nutritious, fiber-rich brown rice has a chewy texture and pleasing taste that can make its colorless cousin second choice. And brown rice cooks easily, although not instantly. As a rule of thumb, use two and a half times as much water as rice. Bring the water to a boil with a little salt (about $1/2$ teaspoon for 1 cup dry rice and $2^1/2$ cups water). Stir rinsed rice into boiling water, reduce heat to low, cover, and let cook slowly for about 35 to 40 minutes.

■ BONUS TIP: *Look into variety rices. Basmati rice is a particularly luscious one. Both brown and white Basmati have a delectable, nutty taste. You can find them in natural foods stores and select supermarkets (I can get the Texmati brand at my neighborhood grocery store). Whatever variety of rice you buy, choose the long-grain type when you want separate grains to serve as a side dish or as a bed for beans or a stir-fry. Short-grain brown rice has a sticky consistency that works well in helping loaves and burgers maintain their shape.*

225. ■ **Short-grain brown rice can even make a fat-free crust** for a quiche or vegetable pie. Cook the rice to be especially sticky by putting it in cold water, bringing it to a boil, then lowering the heat and stirring from time to time. This sticky rice can be pressed into a pie plate and filled. Since you wouldn't put an egg/cream/bacon quiche in such a virtuous crust, consider a tofu quiche. The recipe gets its name because it keeps changing over the years as I learn more. *Mod.*

■ EVOLUTIONARY QUICHE ■

$1/2$ onion, chopped
2 garlic cloves, minced
1 cup chopped spinach, fresh or frozen (thawed)
1 cup mushrooms, sliced
$1^1/2$ pounds firm tofu
1 teaspoon dried marjoram and 1 teaspoon dried dill
      weed
2 teaspoons salt, plus white pepper and ground nutmeg
      to taste
2 tablespoons arrowroot powder
9-inch brown-rice crust

Preheat oven to 350 degrees.

Sauté onion, garlic, spinach, and mushrooms using any oil-free method (I use water with sherry or seasoned rice vinegar). Then set aside. In a food processor, grate $1/2$ pound of the tofu and turn into a medium bowl. With the metal mixing blade in processor, puree the other pound of tofu with the salt.

Then dissolve the arrowroot in either 3 tablespoons water or in 3 tablespoons of the liquid left from sautéing the vegetables. Stir the arrowroot-water mixture into the blended tofu. Stir the vegetables into the blended mixture and add white pepper. Pour into a brown rice crust that has been pressed into a 9-inch pie pan. Bake for approximately 35 minutes. Let sit several minutes after removing from oven to become firm for cutting. ■

Vary the vegetables as you wish: I have successfully used asparagus, broccoli, and zucchini in this quiche instead of mushrooms and spinach. The herbs and spices may be varied as well, and a bit of turmeric can be added for color.

226. ▪ **Give brown rice an almond touch** with this tip from George Mateljan's *Cooking Without Fat:* Instead of using plain water and salt to cook brown rice, boil 2 cups of water with 2 almond tea bags (I use Almond Sunset from Celestial Seasonings). Let the tea steep 10 minutes, remove the bags, return to a boil, add rice, and cook as you usually would.

227. ▪ **Experiment with an array of whole grains** to give body to your meals without high-fat meats and cheeses. Every grain has a unique personality, but one thing you can be sure of with all of them is a negligible fat content. Go beyond those most familiar to us—rice, oats, wheat—and try:

> *millet*—light, fluffy, and so easy to digest
> *kasha*—we also know this Russian staple as buckwheat—
> hearty and flavorful
> *barley*—lovely in soups and on its own, a warming winter
> grain that has sustained the rugged mountain people of Tibet
> for centuries

228. ▪ **Cook rice or other grains in fruit juice** for a subtle sweetness that complements their flavor. A fifty-fifty mixture of apple juice and water works well.

229. ▪ **Vegetable broth** is good for cooking grains and, for that matter, beans as well.

230. ▪ **Celery juice** is another medium for cooking grains. If you have a juicer, you know that straight celery juice tastes too salty to drink, but it's excellent for cooking rice and does away with the need to add either butter or salt. (Thanks to my friend Dr. Ralph Cinque for this tip, which I use frequently.)

231. ▪ **Make a pretty pilaf.** To a rice or barley base, add colorful vegetables: shredded carrot; chopped red, green, and yellow sweet pepper; fresh or frozen peas.

232. ▪ **Save time with boxed grain dishes.** They're sold for use as side dishes, but you can easily give star billing to rice pilaf, barley pilaf, lentil pilaf, and quick-cooking couscous (one easy-to-find brand of all these is Near East). The box directions say to add butter or oil, but the pilafs taste fine with half the amount of oil called for or none at all.

233. ▪ **Use bread crumbs or crushed cereal flakes to top a casserole** instead of cheese or nuts.

234. ▪ **Beans don't take forever to cook, but they do take a while.** For this reason, make a pot of them on the weekend and have the beans available through the week. Soak rinsed beans overnight or boil them for one minute and then soak, covered, for 2 hours. Either way, when you're ready to actually cook the beans, discard the soaking water. Cook the beans in fresh water, 2 to 3 times their volume.

Black beans, great northerns, kidney beans, and pintos cook in $1^1/_2$ to 2 hours; navy beans take about 2 hours; and garbanzos 2 to 3. Little legumes (split peas and lentils) cook in 30 minutes and don't require a presoak. (To fall in love with legumes—and become adept at cooking them while you're at it—see *Romancing the Bean,* by Joanne Saltzman.)

235. ▪ **Investing in one of the new pressure cookers—** they're much improved from the ones you may remember from years ago—can eliminate the presoak and substantially decrease cooking time. With pressure-cooking, you're down to 25 minutes for black, northern, kidney, and pinto beans, 30 minutes for navy beans, and 40 minutes for chick-peas. Most pressure cookbooks recommend adding a tablespoon of oil to the water to keep beans from foaming. You can easily afford to do that with this leanest of all high-protein foods. (One cookbook with an entire chapter on using a pressure cooker for beans is *Recipes from an Ecological Kitchen* by Lorna Sass.)

236. ▪ **Cook beans in large quantities and freeze individual portions** in sandwich bags. For a quick lunch, my friend A.J. suggests thawing a portion of black beans and sautéing them in a small amount of olive oil or in an oil-free medium (see chapter 1). Season with garlic, scallions, and—if you like fiery food—Sichuan bean paste. Roll in a chapati or tortilla and indulge.

237. ▪ **Or keep canned beans in your cupboard.** You can do a lot with them, including borrowing my mom's ultra-easy baked bean recipe.

▪ EASY BEAN BAKE ▪

1 can (16 ounces) each: butter beans, great northern beans, garbanzos, black beans, pinto beans, and kidney beans
2 cups tomato sauce
1 onion, chopped and water-sautéed
2 tablespoons prepared mustard
1 tablespoon barbecue sauce
1 teaspoon dry mustard
$^1/_4$ to $^1/_2$ cup brown sugar to taste

Preheat oven to 350 degrees.

Drain beans and pour them into a very large mixing bowl. Mix other ingredients and carefully stir this sauce into the beans. Pour into a large, oblong baking dish, and bake for 1 hour. Serve hot or cold. (This recipe works with just one kind of beans, of course, or whatever variety you have in the pantry.) ▪

238. ▪ **Replace the ham bone or salt pork in traditional bean dishes** with umeboshi plum, a savory pickled condiment from Japan found at natural foods stores and some Asian markets. Start with just 1 plum (remove before serving) or

1 teaspoon umeboshi plum paste—this is potent stuff. When chef Kathy Hale of Daily Bread in Kansas City first let me in on using this exotic substance with beans, she reminded me that since umeboshi plums are salty, the plum or paste needs to be added near the end of cooking. This is because salt interferes with the beans becoming tender.

■ BONUS TIP: *Legumes' hard-to-shake reputation for causing gas keeps many people from experiencing their gustatory and nutritional benefits. There are many things that can be done to mitigate the gassiness that sometimes accompanies eating beans. One of the most reliable is to throw away the soaking water and cook beans in fresh water, as instructed in tip 234. There is a sugar in the soaking water that is believed to be the culprit.*

Some people also find that using the boil-and-soak method (also in tip 234) rather than an overnight soak is advantageous. Using some of the herb savory to flavor the beans can lessen their gassy effect as well. Processed soy products such as tofu are more readily digested than whole beans, and eating beans as part of a simple meal seems to make them easier to deal with than having them as part of a multicourse banquet. Help is also available from a product called Beano, a few drops of which can counteract any gassiness from beans before you experience it. Find it at health food stores and pharmacies.

PASTA AND PALS

239. ■ **Choose plain flour and water pasta over egg noodles.** Look for the words "semolina" or "durum wheat" on the package; they usually indicate a plain pasta. (This is seldom sold fresh. If you want fresh, eggless noodles, treat yourself to a pasta maker and start from scratch.)

240. ▪ **You don't need to use oil** (or salt for that matter) to cook perfect pasta. Just add the pasta slowly to plenty of boiling water and stir to separate after it's in the pot. Put the sauce on immediately after the pasta is drained so it won't cool and stick together. If you're not serving the pasta right away, you can rinse it before adding the sauce, or toss the sauce with the pasta and return it to the cooking pot to stay warm. (Thanks for this one to West Coast culinary instructor Jia Patton.)

▪ B O N U S   T I P : *Think of pasta when there's not much time to prepare a meal. You can make a green salad while the water boils and heat the sauce and set the table in the few minutes it takes the pasta to cook.*

241. ▪ **Parmesan is a full-fat cheese,** so use it with a light touch, or see if you like sapsago, a sage-flavored cheese made from skim milk. Another alternative is soy Parmesan. Most brands contain about $^1/_3$ the fat of regular dairy Parmesan; Soyco Lite 'N' Less Grated Parmesan is a best-seller among pasta lovers in the food co-op to which I belong. *Mod.*

242. ▪ **Lessen lasagna's fat content** by making vegetable lasagna with spinach, zucchini, or eggplant, and replace ricotta with nonfat cottage cheese moistened with plain, nonfat yogurt (1 part yogurt to 3 parts cottage cheese). For a richer but cholesterol-free "cheese," use crumbled tofu (*mod.*). I often make tofu-vegetable lasagna as a company dish and people eat it up— literally.

243. ▪ **Team your lean, luscious pasta with fat-free garlic bread.** Make this miracle by baking fresh garlic—jumbo-size elephant garlic is great for baking—in a special terra cotta garlic baker (at cookware shops) or other small baking dish. Don't separate the garlic cloves; simply cut the top off the entire bulb and bake at 375 degrees about 25 minutes. The cloves within the bulb will feel soft. Then pop them out and squeeze from them a delectable garlic "butter" to spread on French bread and pop in the toaster oven. (I bake garlic every time I plan to use it, but culinary expert Jennifer Raymond says that baked garlic can be refrigerated in a sealed container for up to 2 weeks.)

244. ▪ **Leftover pasta** should be refrigerated in an airtight container and can be reheated with vegetables of your choice by stirring in a nonstick pan coated with nonstick cooking spray. It can also be stir-fried with oil-free liquids, soy sauce, and vegetables for a Chinese flair. (Leftover rice can be treated in the same ways.)

245. ▪ **Rethink pizza.** With a wonderful red sauce and plenty of veggie toppings, you can make a dynamite pizza without cheese. Use all sorts of toppings—spinach, broccoli, artichoke hearts, soaked sun-dried tomatoes. Even the famous New York pizzerias of Larry "Fats" Goldberg have a cheeseless, all-veggie pizza, the Diet Riot, on their menu. Alternatively, you can use half the mozzarella you used to *(mod.)* or select a fat-free dairy or soy cheese.

246. ▪ **Increase the nutritional value of your pizza crust** by making one that's not only low fat but whole wheat. Use whole wheat pastry flour, not bread flour, to ensure a tender crust, even without oil.

(Note: Refer back to chapter 4 for hints on low-fat pasta sauces.)

POTATO POWER

247. ▪ **For flawless mashed potatoes without butter or milk,** mash steamed potatoes slightly with a fork or hand masher, adding enough water or vegetable broth to facilitate the process, and finish whipping with an electric beater. Add sweet Hungarian paprika, freshly ground pepper, and salt or a pungent salt-free seasoning like Mrs. Dash in amounts to suit you.

248. ■ **Mashed potatoes make a luscious crust** for a vegetable pie without the high-fat content of a pastry crust. For a shepherd's-style pie, simply mix slightly steamed vegetables of your choice (corn, peas, string beans, carrots, sweet red onions) with pepper, salt, and your favorite herbs in a baking dish. Cover with a thick crust of smooth mashed potatoes—mashing with a little extra water or broth will give you the consistency you want for this. Sprinkle paprika on top and bake until hot through. (Cover your pie for a soft potato top; bake uncovered for a chewier, browned crust.)

249. ■ **"Hold the fries"**—well, not necessarily. This recipe for home "fries" comes from Pat Griffin and was printed in *Vegetarian Voice,* the membership journal of the North American Vegetarian Society:

■ **PAT'S HOME FRIES** ■

$^1/_3$ cup onion, shredded or diced fine
$^1/_3$ cup water
3 cups leftover baked or lightly steamed potatoes, chopped fine
Salt and pepper to taste
1 to 2 tablespoons soy sauce

In a large skillet, sauté the onion in the water until it is translucent. Add remaining ingredients. Cook until potatoes are hot. Add $^1/_3$ cup more water if needed. Serve with ketchup, salad, and a green vegetable. ■

250. ■ **Those frozen hash-brown patties** don't have to be fried. Get the ones made with no oil (check the label) and brown them in a nonstick skillet sprayed with nonstick cooking spray to make them audibly crispy. Use medium heat and give them about 12 minutes per side.

251. ▪ **Scalloped potatoes don't sound like light fare,** but they can be. This fat-free, salt-free recipe comes from cookbook author Freya Dinshah:

▪ SCALLOPED POTATOES ▪

1 cup corn, fresh or frozen
1 cup water
2 sticks celery, chopped
1 onion, chopped
2 small bell peppers
3 medium potatoes, peeled and ripple sliced $^1/_4$ inch thick
1 large carrot, ripple sliced $^1/_4$ inch thick
Minced parsley

Preheat oven to 350 degrees.

Make a thin sauce of the corn and water in your blender. Then place vegetables, potatoes, and parsley in the pan in layers, alternating vegetables, potatoes, vegetables, potatoes, parsley. The total depth of food in the pan should be about $1^3/_4$ inches (not more than 2 inches). Bring the corn sauce to a boil, stirring to prevent burning. Pour it evenly over the vegetables. Cover the pan and bake $1^1/_4$ hours. Remove cover. Broil to lightly brown top. ▪

252. ▪ **Bake or steam new potatoes, red potatoes, or yellow Finns** instead of white potatoes. The former varieties retain more moisture and require less doctoring at the table. And yellow Finns even *look* as if they've already been buttered.

253. ▪ **Top a baked potato with a better fat or something better than fat.** If you yearn for something oily on that baker when you swear off butter and margarine, try a little flax seed, olive, walnut, or canola oil, Spectrum Naturals Spread, or mashed avocado (*mod.* for all these). Or experiment freely with the following tater toppers:

254. ▪ **Lemon juice, freshly ground pepper, and salt-free seasoning.**

255. ▪ **Mustard, any kind,** on its own or mixed with a bit of mashed tofu.

256. ▪ **Stir-fried veggies.**

257. ▪ **Steamed mushrooms** (they cook in their own flavorful juices when sealed in foil and placed in a hot oven).

258. ▪ **Baked beans or chili beans.**

259. ▪ **Ratatouille.**

260. ▪ **Creamed corn** (see tip 89).

261. ▪ **Salsa, steak sauce, barbecue sauce, or barbecued onions** (see tip 316).

262. ▪ **Mashed broccoli or cauliflower** (oversteam it so it will mash easily, and use plenty of ground black pepper).

263. ▪ **Mashed sweet potato or yam** (cold leftovers work fine—it's a bit like cold butter on a hot potato).

264. ▪ **Pasta sauce** with plenty of garlic and basil.

265. ▪ **Any low-fat or nonfat gravy** (see chapter 4) **or low-fat or nonfat salad dressing**—particularly the creamy ones (see chapter 3)—with plenty of chives.

266. ▪ **Nonfat commercial sour cream,** or a sour cream stand-in made from blending dry cottage cheese with nonfat buttermilk.

267. ▪ **Soy sour cream,** or a do-it-yourself version made by blending soft tofu with lemon juice and herbs (*mod.*).

268. ▪ **Plain nonfat or soy yogurt.**

269. ▪ **Baked garlic** (see tip 243) and juicy tomato wedges.

270. ▪ **Grated nonfat cheeses,** from which there are now plenty to choose both at the supermarket and health food store; taste varies considerably so test more than one. Several of my friends rave about Soy-a-Melt Fat Free Cheddar and Mozzarella from White Wave.

271. ■ **Or try a spicy specialty from** *The Good Heart Diet Cookbook*, by Judith Stern and Jonathan Michaels:

■ HORSERADISH APPLESAUCE ■

$^1/_2$ cup freshly grated horseradish
2 cups applesauce

Mix to serve with steamed or baked potatoes. *Yield: 1$^1/_2$ cups.* ■

FIESTA FOODS

272. ■ **Refried beans don't even have to be fried the first time:** Simply blend prespiced chili beans in your blender or food processor, or buy canned refries made without lard or oil. We spice up a south-of-the-border buffet at our house with Bearitos Fat Free Refried Beans with Green Chiles from Little Bear Organics.

273. ■ **Buy tortillas made without shortening.** The ingredients list should be simple, that is, corn, lime, and water.

274. ■ **Enjoy unfried tostadas** by baking corn or flour tortillas on a cookie sheet until crisp (about 10 minutes at 375 degrees). They'll be crunchy and ready to top with fillings. (If the edges curl, look for thicker tortillas next time, or place a second cookie sheet on top to keep them flat. (You can also combine cultures and put Mexican toppings on a Middle Eastern pita and save on the fat of a fried tortilla.)

■ BONUS TIP: *A dietitian friend whose clients are largely Hispanic recently reminded me that corn tortillas are a valuable source of calcium. They average 50 milligrams of calcium per tortilla, and it's not difficult to eat several at a sitting.*

275. ▪ **An Irish twist on a Mexican theme:** a *potato burrito.* Add water-sautéed onion and garlic, powdered cumin, and cayenne or jalapeños to piping-hot mashed potatoes. Then roll the mixture in a warmed tortilla with shredded lettuce, chopped tomato and green pepper, and chile salsa.

276. ▪ **Potato tacos are an equally low-fat cross-cultural entree.** Margaret Malone of Milly's Healthful Gourmet Dining in San Rafael has been making these for years. Combine chopped, boiled potatoes with chopped, water-sautéed onions, garlic, and red peppers. Then add capers, currants, and cilantro. Toss with lime juice. In season, fresh corn—uncooked and just cut from the cob—may be folded in at the end, along with some jalapeños for the brave. Serve in a soft taco shell with a fresh tomato salsa.

(Note: For guacamole ideas, see tips 166 and 167.)

MEATS AND EN*LIGHT*ENED ALTERNATIVES

277. ▪ **Change the configuration of your meals** so that when you choose to include meat, it is used as a flavoring instead of the focal point. A robust stew can contain half the meat and twice the carrots and potatoes, and a welcome winter chili can be mostly beans, vegetables, and an impeccably seasoned sauce with just a touch of *carne. Inter.*

278. ▪ **If you eat meat as the main part of an entree, keep the portions small.** In *A Change of Heart: Steps to Healthy Eat-*

ing, the physicians and nutrition experts at the University of Kansas School of Medicine suggest, "A good rule of thumb is to keep your servings of meat no longer than a deck of cards or the palm of your hand, and no thicker than your thumb." This is a serving of 3 ounces or less; slicing it thinly can make it seem like more (*inter.*). Give yourself that satisfied full feeling with grains and vegetables that you can eat in quantity.

    279. ■ **Trim visible fat from meat before cooking,** but remember that much of the fat in meat is "marbled" throughout the cut. *Inter.*

    280. ■ **Stretch a meat loaf or hamburger** with cooked rice, vegetables, mashed potato, or TVP (textured vegetable protein), dry granules that, when reconstituted with water or broth, resemble ground meat. *Inter.*

    281. ■ **Or make "Neat Loaf"** (*mod.*) from Jennifer Raymond's *The Peaceful Palate: Fine Vegetarian Cuisine:*

■ NEAT LOAF ■

1 cup cooked brown rice
1 cup wheat germ
1 cup quick rolled oats *or* oat bran
1 cup finely chopped walnuts *or* sunflower seeds
1 cup chopped mushrooms
1 onion, finely chopped
$1/2$ medium bell pepper, finely chopped
1 medium carrot, shredded or finely chopped
$1/2$ teaspoon *each* of thyme, marjoram, and sage
2 tablespoons soy sauce
2 tablespoons stone ground or Dijon mustard
1 tablespoon peanut butter

(The vegetables should be chopped as finely as possible; a food processor is an invaluable aid in this.) Preheat oven to 350 degrees. Combine all ingredients, and mix for 2 minutes with a large spoon. This will help to bind it together. Pour into a greased 5 × 9-inch loaf pan and bake for 60 minutes, or until lightly browned. You may wish to top the loaf with ketchup after 40 minutes, then return it to the oven to bake the remaining time. Let stand for 10 minutes before serving. *Serves 8 to 10.* ■

Neat Loaf has the look and taste of meat loaf without the meat or grease. It is great topped with ketchup, or wonderful chilled and sliced for sandwiches. The mixture can also be formed into patties and "fried" in a nonstick pan for burgers.

282. ■ **The leanest seafood choices** (*inter.*) are scallops, orange roughy, haddock, sole, cod, shrimp, and crab, all under 1 gram of fat in a $3^{1}/_{2}$-ounce serving. Although many people find it convenient to include fish in their low-fat eating plan, it is not required for health. Grains, legumes, and starchy vegetables are also low in fat. In addition, they're cholesterol free (all fish contain cholesterol, and shellfish have particularly high concentrations). Plant-based entrees also contain far fewer chemical contaminants, and their more moderate protein levels are conducive to strong bones and healthy kidneys.

283. ■ **If pot pie brings back memories** of brisk childhood autumns, reminisce away—without the fatty pie crust. Instead, use a flour tortilla to wrap your pot pie ingredients: potatoes, onions, peas, carrots, and a little chicken (*inter.*), or, better yet, cubed, firm tofu (*mod.*).

284. ■ **Frozen entrees** make life a lot easier, and there are now several to choose from that can meet the low-fat guidelines of the most committed. Read labels carefully and compare the ingredients and the fat content of different brands in the freezers at both your grocery and health food stores. We use a lot of the Legume Italian entrees—lasagna, manicotti, stuffed shells—which use deliciously seasoned tofu (*mod.*) to replace cheese. I also recommend Life Choice entrees from ConAgra, based on the dietary principles of Dr. Dean Ornish, available at select supermarkets.

285. ■ **If you miss something meaty when you make a vegetarian meal,** several products exist to help you miss no more. These include TVP (textured vegetable protein) to use in burgers, chili, loaves, sloppy Joes, and the like. Other "meaty" marvels include:

286. ■ **Seitan,** a meatlike wheat gluten product with almost no fat, that can stand in for meat, poultry, or even fish in stir-fries, casseroles, and stews. If you've ever been to a big-city Chinese restaurant that serves vegetarian versions of everything from Peking duck to electric eel, those amazing facsimiles were made from seitan. (For using seitan in soups, see tip 185.)

287. ■ **Tempeh,** a cultured Indonesian soy product, may have been the inspiration for a time-honored Asian saying, "Honorable soy bean, meat without bones." It comes in blocks that look something like cooked cube steak and has a texture closely resembling that of meat. Although recipes usually suggest frying it in oil, you can marinate and broil it (in your oven or on an outdoor grill), or add it to a stir-fry or casserole. For more information, see *The Book of Tempeh*, by William Shurtleff and Akiko Aoyagi. (*Mod.*—since tempeh is made from soy; fat-reduced tempeh is available at some health food stores.)

288. ■ **Firm tofu** has a somewhat meaty consistency, but its real appeal is its ability to take on the flavor of what is with it, often a savory tamari soy sauce, tomato sauce, or spicy gravy. *Mod.*

289. ■ **Eggplant, mushrooms, and sun-dried tomatoes** are chewy enough to give the mouth-feel of meat without fat or excess protein. Use them in stir-fries, sauces, soups, hefty sandwiches, Italian dishes. I also use soaked, slivered sun-dried tomatoes in spinach salad and on top of crackers as an hors d'oeuvre. (Be sure to buy dried tomatoes dry rather than packed in oil; they're cheaper and have no added fat.)

290. ▪ **Crave a burger?** Look for meatless mixes such as Archer Daniels Midland Burger 'n Loaf Mix, and frozen patties such as "gardenburgers" from Wholesome & Hearty Foods (see tip 441) and Worthington's frozen Morningstar Farm Grillers, meatless burgers at supermarkets nationwide. These average markedly lower in saturated fat and total fat than the leanest hamburgers, and you can keep them that way by frying them without oil in a nonstick pan. These are delicious and totally satisfying burgers. Serve them on buns with ketchup, onion, pickle, and a thick chunk of tomato.

291. ▪ **Or do your veggie burgers from scratch.** For basic burgers, combine mashed cooked legumes (lentils or beans—canned beans are fine) with short-grain brown rice, a little more rice than beans. Add salt, onion powder, and sage or garlic to taste and bake on a nonstick cookie sheet half an hour at 325 degrees. (If you want to add something with the binding quality of an egg, try mashed potato, moistened bread crumbs, or moistened rolled oats.)

292. ▪ **When it's picnic time and you want to grill hot dogs,** note the fat content on the package. Some of the chicken and turkey dogs have as much fat as the beef and pork varieties. The various veggie franks from natural foods stores are another way to go, but they, too, have a wide range when it comes to fat content. If you want your frank to have no fat at all, look into Smart Dogs from Lightlife Foods and Soy Boy Leaner Wieners from Northern Soy. I've enjoyed both of these on warmed hot dog rolls with mustard and relish. We take them to the ball park.

293. ▪ **If you eat turkey on Thanksgiving,** you may know that skinless turkey has about $1/3$ less fat than skinless chicken. But if you're willing to start a new family tradition, you can cut the fat as far as it can go and eliminate cholesterol entirely. In recent years, I've invited family and guests for a holiday meal built around the Stuffed Pumpkin recipe in Mary McDougall's *The McDougall Health-Supporting Cookbook, Vol. 1.* This is a beautiful dish to serve, and it's all the more fun if you make an expedition to the country to pick your pumpkin from a bountiful patch.

■ STUFFED PUMPKIN ■

1 medium pumpkin or large winter squash

Bread stuffing:

1 loaf whole wheat bread
2 cups water
2 onions, chopped
1 tablespoon dried parsley
2 teaspoons thyme
1 teaspoon marjoram
2 teaspoons sage
$1/2$ teaspoon rosemary
2 tablespoons low-sodium tamari (soy sauce)

Cube the bread, place on a baking sheet, and toast in a 300-degree oven for 15 minutes. Combine the remaining stuffing ingredients in a saucepan, bring to a boil, and cook for 15 minutes. Put the toasted bread cubes into a large bowl, add the cooked liquid, and toss well. Cover with a lid or plate for 15 minutes while the cubes absorb the moisture.

Cut off the top of the pumpkin or squash and save for a cover (as if you were going to make a jack-o'-lantern). Clean out seeds and the stringy portion. Place bread stuffing inside, cover with the reserved top. Place in a large roasting pan with

1 inch of water covering the bottom of pan. Bake at 350 degrees for 1^1/$_2$ hours. This makes a good main dish for a festive meal. Serve with mashed potatoes, (fat-free) gravy, assorted steamed vegetables, bread, and a salad. ∎

One thing I especially like about this dish is that you not only get to serve a super stuffing from a lovely pumpkin "tureen," you can also eat the pumpkin. Cold leftover pumpkin is tasty tossed with lemon juice, garlic powder, and salt.

VEGETABLES SIDE AND CENTER

294. ∎ **Vegetables that are fresh and in season** taste great and don't cry out for butter and salt like old, flavorless ones do. Shop at farmers' markets when you can and if you're a gardener (or friendly with a generous one), so much the better. Many people also swear by the taste superiority of organically grown produce.

295. ∎ **Cook vegetables in fruit juices** for a delicately sweet flavor in a side dish or as a nice addition to a low-fat casserole. Orange juice is a good choice for many vegetables, turnips and carrots among them.

296. ∎ **Serve tender, young asparagus with lemon wedges.** Skipping the traditional Hollandaise sauce will save you 18 grams of fat in a typical serving.

297. ∎ **On greens and stronger-tasting vegetables,** use a touch of fruited or balsamic vinegar. Garlic is also a natural on those superhealthful dark, leafy greens. Wash fresh collards, kale, or mustard greens and let some of the water cling to the leaves so an ample sprinkling (or two or three) of garlic powder will stick and you can steam the greens over water or in a bit of vegetable broth. Salt to taste. (One study showed that, among people with healthy lifestyles who outlive the expected norm, those who live longest of all are the ones who consume the most leafy greens.)

298. ■ **Make a robust vegetable stew based on starchy vegetables** of your choice: potatoes, yams, rutabaga, winter squash. Use an onion or two, and leeks or shallots if you like, and later in the cooking process add lighter vegetables—asparagus, green beans, zucchini, broccoli florets. Use the herbs and seasonings you prefer. I put sage and thyme in vegetable stew.

299. ■ **Stir-fried vegetables, served with rice or noodles,** make an entree with or without the addition of a concentrated protein food. Using a wok means you can get by with a very small amount of oil since the oil stays in the center where you can easily stir around your garlic, ginger, etc. You'll need so little oil that even pungent, pricy sesame oil can be used for the purpose. Heat the oil (less than 1 tablespoon) first so the food won't absorb it. When the basic seasonings have browned, add about 2 tablespoons of water (or 1 tablespoon water and 1 tablespoon Chinese rice wine). *Watch out for the big cloud of steam.* As the liquid evaporates, add about 2 tablespoons more water and put the lid on the wok. You will, in effect, be steaming the rest of your dish, but you'll have the luscious flavor of the seasonings carried by the oil.

■ BONUS TIP: *For a successful stir-fry, pay attention to your chopping techniques. Cutting on the diagonal is ideal since you expose more of the food to the heat that way. Cut the vegetables into small pieces for quick cooking; in this case, small pieces are not just convenient, they're the essence of the process. Vegetables that take a longer time to cook (carrots, for instance) can be briefly steamed or blanched before going into the stir-fry.*

300. ▪ **Some vegetables cook nicely in the oven** on a pan coated with nonstick cooking spray. Small, tender zucchini, quartered lengthwise, can be placed on a sprayed baking sheet, salted and peppered, and sprayed again with just a touch of nonstick cooking spray on top—it will give the veggies a wonderful brown crispness. Bake in a fast oven—400 degrees—but watch closely; these take only 4 or 5 minutes to be done and they can burn after that. Be careful not to overcook; the zucchini should retain a little crispness. (Thanks for this to Mildred Aissen.)

301. ▪ **Veggies on the grill**—is a delicious way to enjoy these colorful, nutritious foods. Virginia Messina, M.P.H., R.D., co author of *The No-Cholesterol Vegetarian Barbecue Cookbook*, suggests marinating vegetables in a mixture of soy sauce and a little lemon juice, olive oil, and fresh herbs. For a totally fat-free marinade, replace the olive oil with vegetable broth.

It's ideal to allow the vegetables to soak up the marinade for an hour or two, and steaming the vegetables for a minute or two first will help them take on the flavors more easily. But for a quick summer dinner, simply brush the vegetables of your choice with marinade and head for the grill. Vegetables that take best to grilling include eggplant, summer squash, bell pepper, corn, tomatoes, potatoes, and onions.

302. ▪ **Roasting enhances the flavor of vegetables and uses minimal oil.** To do this, toss colorful, seasonal vegetables—sweet red pepper, broccoli, carrot, kohlrabi—in just enough garlic-laced oil to glaze. Roast in a preheated cast-iron skillet over high heat for 5 minutes or less, stirring occasionally. Remove from the heat, toss with a bit of fresh lime juice and coarsely ground black pepper. This is a beautiful way to "eat your veggies." (Thanks for this to Kathy Hale of Daily Bread, Kansas City.)

CHAPTER 6

Get the Fat Out of Sandwiches, Snacks, and Appetizers

Casual foods—the sandwich on the run, the munchies with TV, the pâté at the cocktail party—make a major contribution to many diets. We all eat them. We all like them. And most of us feel we'd be better off with fewer of them. It's true that many of the fattiest foods in the American diet—processed luncheon meats, high-fat cheeses, mayonnaise, roasted nuts, chocolate bars, and salty, oily chips—fall into this category.

But just because something is eaten before a meal, outside a meal, or between two pieces of bread does not mean that it has to be a dietary derelict. We simply need to make sound choices every time we put something in our mouths, whether at a bona fide sit-down meal or somewhere else. What is important in getting the fat out of our diets is what foods we eat, not when we eat them or where or with what utensils (if indeed we're using utensils at all).

Sandwiches start out with something to recommend them because they're based on bread, a staple, low-fat food. Give yourself the advantage of fiber by choosing whole-grain bread when you have the chance, and make it a really tasty bread that doesn't need to be slathered with margarine or mayo. Be willing to explore lighter spreads and uncommon fillings for sand-wiches that will make you happy that it's lunchtime, even on days you're not at work.

Snacks are defined as anything eaten between meals. Some people do better with no snacks at all; they like the rhythm of regular mealtimes and having a keen appetite at each one. Those who have had trouble with overeating often find that having set times to eat and sticking with them is a real help.

Other folks are natural grazers. They would rather eat small meals or snacks as they go along than three squares a day. And when you cut the fat in your diet, you may feel the need for a midmorning snack and one in the afternoon simply because low fat foods don't "stick to your ribs" for hours on end. This is really a good thing—after all, low-fat foods aren't sticking to your arteries either.

It's perfectly acceptable to respond to the legitimate desire for food by eating healthful, low-fat foods more frequently. In fact, unless you're capable of eating large quantities at a sitting, snacks can be indispensable when you're aiming for a daily min-imum of five servings of grains and three each of vegetables and fruits.

Appetizers and hors d'oeuvres needn't jeopardize your fat-cutting resolutions either. The chapters dealing with salads, soups, and desserts can be of help when you're looking for appropriate first courses and party fare. And this chapter will give you even more ideas for taking the edge off an appetite deliciously, graciously, and healthfully.

■ ■ ■

SANDWICH SPREADS AND FILLERS

303. ▪ Use mustard, ketchup, or barbecue sauce instead of mayonnaise on sandwiches. Mustard is not fat free, but it's so pungent, moderation is a given. Become a mustard connoisseur and try the ones spiked with wine, miso, or horseradish.

304. ▪ Perk up nonfat mayo with a dash of hot pepper sauce.

305. ▪ Ground raw, hulled sunflower seeds added to plain nonfat or soy yogurt with a bit of harissa, the hot Middle Eastern condiment, makes a good spread with an interesting texture. *Mod.*

306. ▪ Make a sandwich spread with soft tofu. Mash the tofu with enough nonfat or soy mayo to make a spread, and add onion and soy sauce, garlic powder, and freshly ground pepper to taste. Serve on your favorite bread with lettuce, tomato, and crisp pickle slices. *Mod.*, unless you use special low-fat tofu.

307. ▪ Get moistness in your sandwiches without fat by using juicy vegetables like cucumber and tomato slices. If you're brown-bagging that sandwich, be sure that lettuce or onion comes between that succulent tomato slice and the bread so you won't end up with a soggy staff of life. (You could also pack the tomato separately.)

308. ▪ Replace high-fat luncheon meats with lower-fat choices. The ones that often get between two slices of sourdough at my house are Smart Deli Thin Slices from Lightlife Foods and Yves Veggie Deli Slices from Yves Fine Foods of Vancouver. Both are meatless, meatlike, and absolutely fat free.

309. ▪ A novel but uncomplicated sandwich idea was

given to me by A. F. Piper, the gentleman in whose taxi I rode one afternoon in Washington, D.C.: Roast a seasoned, ripe eggplant in its own juices and use the resultant soft meat of the eggplant as a spread for bread or stuffing for a pita pocket.

To season the eggplant, puncture the skin in 3 or 4 places and insert a peeled garlic clove into each hole. Then wrap the eggplant in foil and roast it at 350 degrees until the skin is blackened and the inside is very soft. Remove the garlic cloves and the charred skin. Then mash the eggplant with as much chopped raw onion and salt and pepper as you'd like for additional flavoring. Serve with toast or pita. (In India, people eat this for breakfast.) You can do something similar using tomato instead of eggplant; just leave out the garlic.

310 ■ **Decrease the fat of your peanut butter sandwich** by whipping in an almost equal amount of water to emulsify the peanut butter. This gives it more volume and easier spreadability so we can get peanut flavor for the kid in all of us while using less peanut butter and subsequently less fat. Put the spread on one slice of bread, fruit jam on the other. Some people like sliced banana on peanut butter sandwiches. I prefer cool, crunchy lettuce. *Mod.*

311. ■ **Garbanzos and peanut butter combine** for a fat-reduced spread, too. Mix natural peanut butter half and half with pureed, cooked or canned garbanzos. (Be sure the peanut butter has been out of the refrigerator an hour or so before you do this so you don't have to build your biceps in order to do the mixing. A food processor helps if you're making enough for more than one sandwich. *Mod.*)

312. ■ **Garbanzo beans can also make a butter** without a nut in sight. This recipe comes from *The Pritikin Program for Diet & Exercise,* by Nathan Pritikin and Patrick McGrady, Jr.:

■ ■ ■

■ GARBANZO "NUT BUTTER" ■

4 cups cooked garbanzo beans
2 tablespoons cornstarch
$1/3$ cup frozen apple juice concentrate, thawed
1 tablespoon vanilla extract
1 tablespoon ground cinnamon
$1^1/_2$ cups liquid from cooking beans

Cook garbanzo beans until almost but not completely tender.
Drain, saving $1^1/_2$ cups of cooking liquid. Place beans in a single layer in a nonstick baking pan in a 350-degree oven, stirring occasionally to toast evenly, for about $1^1/_2$ hours. Grind toasted garbanzos in a food processor or blender.

Blend cornstarch, apple juice, vanilla, and cinnamon to a smooth mixture. Mix in garbanzo bean liquid. Heat mixture in a saucepan over low heat, stirring constantly until thickened. Stir thickened mixture into the ground toasted garbanzos. Use as stuffing for celery sticks for appetizers, or spread on bread or crackers for a snack or sandwich. ■

313. ■ **Give a sandwich some character**—and not a fat character—by replacing some of the expected lettuce with more outspoken vegetables: mixed baby greens (the ones that include arugula, cilantro, endive), crunchy water chestnuts, spicy sprouts (fenugreek, radish, red clover), green chiles, a slice of Vidalia onion.

314. ■ **Baked eggplant** makes a dandy sandwich filling. Preheat oven to 350 degrees. Slice the eggplant about $1/_2$-inch thick. With 1 tablespoon of low-fat pasta sauce spread on each slice, bake on a cookie sheet sprayed with nonstick cooking spray for about half an hour. (Thanks for this to Muriel Collura.)

315. ■ **And caponata, a saucy Italian eggplant dish,** makes a heroic hero on a kaiser roll. Start by browning cubed eggplant pieces on both sides under the broiler (use some non-stick cooking spray or a little olive oil). Then mix with a toothsome tomato sauce (don't skimp on the garlic or basil), capers (a natural any time you cook eggplant or tomatoes), and (optional) sliced mushrooms sautéed in vegetable broth or red wine.

316. ▪ **Barbecued onions** make any sandwich worth a second helping. Sauté the onions—sweet Italian onions work well here—in a small amount of oil or other liquid (see chapter 1 on fat-free sautéing) with a little soy sauce. When the onions are almost tender, stir in your favorite low-fat barbecue sauce and finish cooking. These are good on burgers of all sorts and in pita bread with raw and sautéed vegetables and/or a bean dip or spread.

317 ▪ **The British know their veggie sandwiches.** For a cucumber sandwich, soak the cucumber slices in red wine vinegar for a few minutes and layer them on thinly sliced bread. (Cut into triangles for tea sandwiches—popular among young children, dolls, and teddy bears.)

318. ▪ **A watercress sandwich** is made by spreading nonfat or soy mayonnaise (*mod.*) on your favorite toast and adding the nutritious watercress. (Wash it well and, if you're patient, remove the stems.)

319. ▪ **A "salad sandwich"**—I had my first in England on a train between London and Brighton—is just what it says: a salad on bread. The traditional British salad sandwich is on white bread with mayo, but you can do a salad sandwich on any bread—whole wheat, rye, a burger bun, or a pita pocket—and add any spread: mustard, salsa, nonfat or soy mayonnaise (*mod.*), even a thin layer of steak sauce. Take your pick of vegetables: leaf lettuce, grated carrot, sprouts, sliced mushrooms, radishes, even cold steamed broccoli. Drained water chestnuts or slices of leftover cooked potato add a bit of extra substance.

THE SNACK CART

320. ■ **Fruit is the most suitable snack in existence.** It's handy, virtually fat free, packed with nutrients, and juicy so you don't need a drink with it. Audrey Cross, Ph.D., of the Institute of Human Nutrition at Columbia University, did a study on snacking habits in the U.S. Among her findings was that only 19 percent of Americans regularly snack on fruit.

321. ■ **Dried fruit can satisfy a snacker's sweet tooth** so there's no need to resort to a high-fat candy bar. Big Medjool dates are my favorites, but dried pineapple, apricots, papaya, and even raisins do the job, too. (These foods, although low in fat, have high concentrations of natural sugars, so they're best not used indiscriminately.)

■ B O N U S T I P : *Look for dried fruit that does not contain sulfur dioxide as a preservative. The bright color of the fresh fruit won't be preserved, but with all the artificial chemicals we eat and breathe in our modern world, this is an easy way to avoid one more.*

322. ■ **Raw veggies snack well, too.** You can't beat them for fat content (almost none) and if you keep some washed and sliced in your fridge in airtight containers, they're fast food in the finest sense of the term. Besides, eating them gives you that superior feeling of doing something unabashedly healthful. (Refer to chapter 3 for suggestions on dips.)

323. ■ **Crackers, like vegetables, are compatible with dips and salsa.** Some fat-free crackers that may not be great by themselves take beautifully to such toppings.

324. ■ **Think Scandinavian** when you're shopping for crackers, since those classics (Ry-Krisp, Wasabrod, and the like) have always been lower in fat than most others, and they're delicious alone or with spreads.

325. ▪ **Saltines were what the word "cracker" meant to me growing up,** and Nabisco Fat-Free Premium Crackers are saltines with $1/3$ less salt and no fat at all. These are great buddies for soup or a spread.

326. ▪ **Rice cakes were considered hippie food** when they were introduced, but they're standard, fat-free fare today. Plain, unsalted rice cakes don't taste like much unless you add a sweet or savory spread or even a few shakes of soy sauce. The lightly salted rice cakes are fine on their own, however, as are the many flavored ones now at the supermarket. Read the labels; a few flavors lose their low-fat identity. And be creative about dressing up rice cakes. Little kids love to make faces on them with raisins and date pieces, sweet red pepper and grated carrot, apple and mandarin orange slices. Employ your sense of fun and your children's.

327. ▪ **A sweet snack to delight in** is a rice cake "ice cream sandwich." Use full-size (not mini) rice cakes to sandwich a thick slice of nonfat frozen yogurt or a nondairy frozen dessert like the nonfat Sweet Nothings or very low-fat Living Lightly. These sandwiches are cold, crunchy, and creamy all at once—heavenly. (There's a whole section on frozen treats in chapter 7.)

328. ▪ **Chips are contemporary Americana,** although their nutritional reputation is less than exemplary. Lots of low-fat and fat-free varieties are on the market, but the chips that I buy literally by the case are Popsters from American Grains. These are baked potato chips with no oil added. You can find them at both grocery and natural foods stores. They're so good that my agent sent a bag of them to every publisher to whom she presented the proposal for this book to show them how terrific fat-free versions of old favorites can be.

329. ▪ **"I'll have a pretzel."** Good choice: you just saved yourself 51 percent of the fat of conventional potato chips.

330. ▪ **Popcorn can be the paragon of sinless snacks.** It smells good, everybody likes it, and an air popper or microwave oven with a special air-popper bowl makes it possible to enjoy popcorn that's virtually fat free, as compared with 36 grams of fat in a 12-cup bowl of oil-popped corn. You can do oil-free popcorn in a covered pan, too, if the pan is quite heavy and you shake it like the dickens.

331. ▪ **Spray popcorn with a fine water mist** to help powdered seasonings (like cheesy nutritional yeast flakes or a sprinkling of garlic, onion, or chili powder) stick. You can also mist your popcorn with the finest spray of extra-virgin olive oil (*mod.*) from a pump bottle.

332. ▪ **Tamari soy sauce is divine on air-popped corn,** supplanting both butter and salt. And since it adds a little wetness, it helps powdered seasonings stick, too. Drip on cautiously or use a spray bottle.

333. ▪ **Drizzle honey or molasses** over plain, air-popped corn. It's like caramel corn you can eat with a spoon.

334. ▪ **Chestnuts roasting on an open fire**—or baked in your oven—are one way to have nuts to munch and stay fat free. To roast them, make a slit on one side of each nut and bake for an hour at 400 degrees. Another way to do this is to roast the slit nuts in a skillet over high heat, shaking vigorously as you would for popcorn, and letting the skins get nearly black. Peel and eat as snacks. (Chestnuts have a unique nature in that, unlike other nuts, they're starchy instead of oily. Their flavor is distinctive, too, and not to be missed.)

335. ▪ **Toasted chick-peas** can be eaten like nuts. Heat drained, cooked or canned garbanzos on the tray in the toaster oven for 5 minutes and top with your favorite seasoning, such as Spike, Mrs. Dash, or Eden Organic Sesame Shake. (Thanks to Stan Rosenfeld for this tip.)

336. ▪ **Toast rolled oats**—old-fashioned, not quick-cooking—on a cookie sheet in the oven, stirring every now and then until the oats get crunchy. This makes a simple snack that, if you have a willing imagination, may remind you of sunflower seeds.

337. ▪ **Make your own nonfat ice pops** by freezing fruit juice in the plastic frozen treat containers you can buy at any supermarket. (Commercial Popsicles are fat free as well.)

338. ▪ **I had my first "banana pop-stick"** one hot August day at a Medieval Faire, and they've become a summer standby. Impale a small, peeled banana (or half a large one) on an ice cream stick and freeze overnight. You can roll the banana in roasted carob powder for a chocolate flavor before freezing if you like. (I realize there were no freezers and few bananas in medieval Europe, but when it's a humid 90 degrees out, historical accuracy becomes a secondary concern.)

APPETIZERS AND HORS D'OEUVRES

339. ▪ **The prettiest warm weather aperitif** I know of is melon cream. (See tip 115.) For a stunning table when you entertain, make a rainbow of melon creams in stemmed goblets—pale green honeydew at one place, inviting orange cantaloupe for the next person, cheery pink watermelon for the third.

340. ▪ **Absolutely fresh vegetable and fruit juices** are another way to lightly introduce a meal. Some stores sell fresh apple and carrot juices made daily, but the juice you make in your own juice extractor and serve immediately is better. The combinations are endless.

341. ▪ **Serve fresh mushrooms marinated** in an oil-free vinaigrette (see "Dressed for Success" in chapter 3).

342. ▪ **Chinese appetizers needn't be fried.** Egg rolls can be baked in a hot oven (450 degrees) for 12 to 15 minutes, until they're golden brown.

343. ▪ **Toss cold noodles** with Thailandish Peanut Sauce (tip 216—*mod.*) for a rich-tasting first course that's not overly abundant in fat. (Keep the rest of the meal oil free by serving succulent vegetables, rice, and a tempting fruit tray for dessert.)

344. ▪ **A croustade, in addition to being a lovely little French word,** is a lovely little cup for enclosing hot hors d'oeuvres rather than using fatty pastry shells. My mom taught me to make croustades by cutting the crusts from sliced bread (white works best) and rolling the sliced bread with a rolling pin until it's as thin as piecrust. Then cut the rolled-out bread into rounds that will cozily fit in nonstick or sprayed muffin tins. For hot hors d'oeuvres, stuff and bake as long as the filling requires. For something uncooked, bake empty croustades in a slow oven—about 250 degrees—until they're golden (10 minutes may be enough); then fill.

345. ▪ **Or let mushroom caps make a veggie vessel** with which to stuff a mixture of toasted bread crumbs moistened with tomato sauce or sherry and seasoned with salt, pepper, and your favorite herbs and spices. Place the stuffed caps on a cookie sheet and bake in a preheated hot oven (425 or so) until the mushrooms are tender.

346. ▪ **Barbecued bean spread** is a guest-pleasing appetizer with crackers. Drain and coarsely puree a can of your favorite beans (pintos, red beans, great northerns) and mix with 5 to 6 tablespoons of barbecue sauce and $1/8$ teaspoon of cayenne. (This is good for sandwiches, too.)

347. ▪ **Bread sticks** will tame the hunger demon until dinner is served. Commercial bread sticks work fine with dip, or make hot bread stick hors d'oeuvres by spreading whole-grain or rye bread with a thin coating of Spectrum Naturals

Spread (*mod.*) or reconstituted Butter Buds and spicing with Cajun seasoning powder, dried dill weed and tarragon, parsley flakes, garlic powder, salt and salt-free seasoning, and a few soy bacon-flavored bits. Cut bread into 1-inch fingers and toast in toaster oven.

If you're making these in quantity, lightly toast the bread first, then place the prepared bread sticks under the broiler for about 1 minute only. (My daughter always makes these when we have parties. They're definite crowd-pleasers.)

348. ▪ **Make a relish tray your guests will really relish** by selecting bright, color-contrasting vegetables: broccoli next to cauliflower, red bell pepper rings around cucumber slices, red and yellow tomato wedges making a fan on the platter. Combine textures, too, by including cold, lightly steamed asparagus and string beans in the arrangement, and have some dill pickle spears, pickled beets, and baby corn as piquant accents. Garnish with radish roses and carrot curls to turn an ordinary vegetable tray into an extraordinary one in no time.

CHAPTER 7

Get the Fat Out of Baking, Desserts, and Treats

Our society has a bizarre relationship with baked goods and sweets. We call them treats but also temptations, delicious but decadent. Every suburban women's group has passed around some recipe called "Better Than Sex Cake," but there's no "Better Than Sex Spaghetti Sauce" or "Better Than Sex Pâté."

Because desserts conjure up such mixed emotions of love and fear, there is probably nowhere except a five-year-old's birthday party that you can find people eating ice cream and cake without a vague sense of engaging in sin. One answer to this sweet schizophrenia is to choose desserts and bakery products that taste as good as they're supposed to with less fat than expected. And if there's a little less sugar there, too—well, that's extra credit.

It's natural for human beings to like sweet things. Our first food, mother's milk, is quite sweet, and the yearning for sweetness may have led early humans to seek out fruit with its abundance of nutrients. Refined sugar is not an ideal way to satisfy this drive; it doesn't give us any vitamins, minerals, protein, fiber, complex carbohydrate, or anything else we expect from food short of gustatory entertainment. Nevertheless, it's when sugar joins forces with fat that the trouble really starts.

When you talk with reformed "sugar junkies," they'll tell you that they didn't binge on hard candies or sugar cubes—plain, unadulterated sugar—but rather on cookies and pies and chocolates, that is, fat/sweet combinations. Although some people have medical conditions requiring the curtailment of all sweets, removing the fat from desserts is all it takes for most people to be able to enjoy them in reasonable amounts without ill effects or an insatiable craving for more. Nevertheless, learning to appreciate low-fat sweets may require some reeducation of the palate.

Since I seldom eat oily, sugary things anymore, I love the ambrosial quality of fresh fruit and other understated desserts. But when I was a candy-and-cookie-crazed youngster I thought that eating fruit was punishment and that people who put apples in kids' trick-or-treat bags were ogres who didn't like children. That's not to say that I never fancy a piece of cake or a cookie or something cold and creamy from the freezer. When I do, I'm glad to be living now when scores of these goodies exist in nonfat and low-fat forms.

There is also a great deal of information on ways to bake at home without using eggs, butter, or oil. I cannot honestly tell you to expect from nonfat baking results identical to those you get when using lots of shortening. Flaky pastry, for example, is by definition high-fat pastry. What you can expect from oil-free baking is a heartier, more substantial product. It's good, but it may be a bit different from what you're used to.

If you're still thinking about flaky pastries (or butterscotch sundaes or holiday cookies or banana cream pies) and saying, "No, I'll never give them up!" take heart. Provided your health is good and you eat a truly low-fat diet—remember whole grains, vegetables, fruits, and legumes—you can indulge on a special occasion in the rich dessert you're passionate about. After all, treats are treats because they're not an everyday occurrence.

It is also true, however, that as you eat lighter fare for longer and longer periods, you will come to prefer it. And from the very start, low-fat goodies like those on the pages to follow can be mouth-watering delicacies that you can have *often* without making excuses or exceptions. As a bonus, when you use natural ingredients such as fresh fruits and whole grains, you're actually adding to your daily nutritional quotient rather than detracting from it. This is the way to placate your taste buds *and* every cell in your body—all seventy-three trillion of them.

FABULOUS FRUITS

349. ■ **Present fruit as something special** so it won't seem like some kind of second-class diet dessert. Serve fresh strawberries with their stems attached and confectioners' sugar for dipping. Broil grapefruit with tupelo honey or pure maple syrup drizzled over the top and a cherry in the center. Layer seasonal fruits in a graceful compote glass and separate the layers with Mock Whipped Cream (tip 392).

■ BONUS TIP: *Locally grown fresh fruit in season is nutritious, reasonably priced, and should be an important part of everyone's diet. But there's nothing like an unusual or out-of-season fruit to give you that vacation feeling right at home. You can either spend two hours' wages on an imported melon in February, or you can freeze appropriate fruits when they are cheap and plentiful and serve them at an unexpected time. And don't forget the appeal of exotic, tropical fruits: mango, papaya, cherimoya, star fruit.*

350. ▪ **Apples when they're baking smell like the richest dessert on earth,** but they can easily contain no added fat whatsoever. Peel the top halves of your favorite cooking apples (Jonathan, Rome beauty, winesap) and take out the cores. If you like, you can stuff the cored space with raisins or chopped dates. Pour on honey or New England maple syrup and bake for about an hour, adding more syrup as necessary to keep the apples moist. These are yummy hot or cold, and your house will hold the lovely scent for hours.

351. ▪ **Freeze grapes** and serve them elegantly in a brandy snifter or eat them casually out of hand. These are surprisingly delicious and when the weather is hot, they act as edible air conditioning.

352. ▪ **If I'm not eating a rich dessert,** I at least want a dessert that makes me feel rich. These Poached Bananas from *The Good Heart Diet Cookbook,* by Judith Stern and Jonathan Michaels, do just that.

▪ **POACHED BANANAS** ▪

6 firm bananas
$1/4$ cup orange juice concentrate
1 cup dry white wine
1 stick cinnamon

Peel the bananas and set aside. Combine the other ingredients with 1 cup water and bring to a boil. Simmer 5 minutes. Add the bananas to the liquid and cook at a bare simmer for 5 minutes. Allow them to sit 15 minutes in the liquid before serving. *Serves 6.* ▪

▪ BONUS TIP: *When you eat a mango, be sure it's very soft (you can get them at a discount on the quick sale table when they're at their peak of ripeness). Break off the part of the fruit where the stem was attached and give the mango a firm squeeze to extract a small stream of juice. In Indian tradition, it is believed that this reduces the acidity in the fruit and makes it taste sweeter.*

353. ▪ **If you're searching for a truly festive dessert,** this will serve your needs handsomely—and because it's from Mary McDougall, it's fat free (*The McDougall Health Supporting Cookbook, Vol. 1*):

▪ CAROB FRUIT FONDUE ▪

1 tablespoon roasted carob powder
2 teaspoons cornstarch or arrowroot
2 tablespoons water
1 can (6 ounces) apple juice concentrate, thawed
1 teaspoon vanilla
2 cups mixed fresh fruit, cut in chunks

Combine the carob powder and cornstarch or arrowroot in a small saucepan. Gradually add the water to make a smooth paste. Stir in the apple juice concentrate. Cook over low heat, stirring constantly until thickened. Stir in the vanilla. Place the sauce in a fondue pot or chafing dish to keep warm for dipping. Dip pieces of fresh fruit into the warm sauce. Try chunks of bananas, apples, pineapple, honeydew melon, or cantaloupe. ▪

354. ▪ **When a fruit salad becomes a gel,** it stops being a low-fat salad and becomes a low-fat dessert. I make gels with agar flakes, which you can buy at any health food store. Simply dissolve 1 tablespoon of the flakes in 2 cups of hot fruit juice. Pour this over your fruit salad ingredients (or even over a single fruit like peach or pear pieces, sliced banana, or fresh berries). Chill to set.

355. ▪ **An epicurean dessert with no fat** is Brandied Dried Fruits from *Fast and Low: Easy Recipes for Low-Fat Cuisine,* by Joan Stillman:

■ BRANDIED DRIED FRUITS ■

$1^1/_2$ cups dried apricots, pears, prunes, raisins, or other
    fruit
1 tablespoon honey
$^3/_4$ cup (or more) brandy

Cover dried fruit with boiling water and let stand 5 minutes.
Drain. Trickle honey over the fruit and mix in. Fill clear glass
jars 7/8 full with the fruit. Top off each jar with brandy (cheap
brandy will do fine) and seal them tight. Use them to top cut-
up bananas, oranges, and grapefruit in late winter. Flavor
improves with time. These fruits, in attractive jars, would make
fine Christmas presents. ■

Note: Be sure to refer to other suggestions for using fruit in
chapter 2.

TIPS FOR BETTER BAKING

356. ■ **When a recipe calls for only one egg,** you can in
most cases just leave it out. You can also avoid the colossal
cholesterol content of egg yolk by using two egg whites (*inter.*)
for each egg called for, or substitute for each egg any of the
following:

357. ■ **One-quarter cup tofu** blended with the liquid used
in the recipe.

358. ■ **Or one-half banana, mashed.**

359. ■ **Or one-quarter cup applesauce.**

360. ■ **Or one-quarter cup canned pumpkin.**

361. ■ **Or commercial egg replacer:** $1^1/_2$ teaspoons of egg replacer powder mixed thoroughly with 2 tablespoons of water will work where one egg did before. The brand I see most often is Ener-G.

362. ▪ **You can simply eliminate up to one third of the fat** in almost any baked good without a flavor change in the finished product.

363. ▪ **Choose white cake flour or whole wheat pastry flour** for baking anything other than yeast breads. Fat makes baked goods more tender by breaking down the wheat protein (gluten). Since cake and pastry flours have less gluten than bread flour does, you can bake with no butter or oil without this being a handicap. (Overbeating causes more gluten to develop in flour, so stir ingredients just enough to mix them well, no more.)

364. ▪ **Using honey as your sweetener** adds thickness and moisture that may be lacking when you leave out fat. Other more unusual liquid sweeteners provide these same qualities. I have baked with brown rice syrup, barley malt, sorghum, maple syrup, cane syrup, fruit juice concentrates, and light and dark molasses. Each gives its own subtle flavor along with its sweetness.

365. ▪ **The name may sound awful—***prune paste***—**but this humbly titled mixture can be used to replace up to 75 percent of the oil or shortening in muffins, brownies, or whatever else you're baking. That's a 75 percent reduction in fat and most people can't tell the difference in the finished product. A 1991 *Washington Post* article gave these easy instructions for making prune paste: Blend 1 cup pitted prunes with 6 tablespoons water and 2 teaspoons vanilla. Use it in the same amounts you'd use of butter, oil, etc., for up to three quarters of the amount called for. It's best fresh, but it can be kept refrigerated for several days. (Some people I know use prune baby food straight from the jar for this—no mixing or blending.)

366. ■ **Another easy fat substitute is applesauce.** Use it measure for measure to replace oil in baking. (Mashed banana works, too, but it affects flavor so is only recommended for those breads, muffins, or cookies in which a hint of banana would be welcome.)

367. ■ **Pureed tofu can substitute for two thirds of the butter or oil** in a cake or cookie recipe. Using 2 ounces of tofu instead of half a stick of butter saves a whopping 43 grams of largely saturated fat. (Note: Since tofu, banana, and applesauce can substitute for eggs as well as for butter or oil, you'll need to experiment with each recipe when you're replacing both.)

368. ■ **Pureed corn cut from the cob** is the serendipitous substitute for fat in some baking that Margaret Malone discovered when she was teaching a food-preparation class during sweet corn season. The corn adds fiber, complex carbohydrate, and a delicate sweetness. Puree it thoroughly (a food processor enables you to do this without water), but since you won't get a completely smooth result, use this in baked goods where extra texture would add to rather than detract from the effect you want. Measure the pureed corn as you would have measured the oil or butter.

369. ■ **An extra teaspoon of baking powder or baking soda** added to whatever you bake helps ensure that your fat-reduced bakery product will rise properly.

370. ■ **Doing eggless and/or shortening-free baking** requires a really accurate oven temperature. If you're not sure of yours, check it with an oven thermometer on a center rack. Let the thermometer "bake" about 15 minutes and check to see that it matches the oven setting.

371. ■ **Use half the nuts** or coconut called for in the recipe (*mod.*), or make your own "nuts" with this recipe from *Just No Fat*, by Norman Rose:

■ MOCK BLACK WALNUTS ■

$^1/_4$ cup TVP (textured vegetable protein)
1 tablespoon black walnut flavoring extract

Combine ingredients, cover, and let sit for at least an hour. Use in recipes calling for black walnuts, such as brownies. For "almonds," use almond flavoring extract. ■

372. ■ **You don't need to oil measuring cups and spoons** to keep liquid sweeteners from sticking to them. Instead spray the utensils with a nonstick cooking spray.

PIES AND PUDDINGS

373. ■ **Pie can be crustless** (the crust is where most of the fat is found) as long as the filling is firm. Pumpkin pie, for example, can stand up without crust (and tofu replaces eggs well in this autumn classic). You can also serve a very light, all-fruit "pie" without a crust. This recipe comes from Freya Dinshah's *The Vegan Kitchen*. She calls her recipe Blueberry Pudding but since it's made in a pie pan and is served sliced in wedges, I've taken the liberty of calling it

■ FREYA'S NO-CRUST BLUEBERRY PIE ■

1 pint fresh (or thawed frozen, unsweetened) blueberries
10 pitted dates
4 ripe bananas

Wash blueberries (if fresh) and blend them in blender with the dates until smooth. Then peel the bananas and slice them into a pie dish. Pour the blueberry-date mixture over the bananas. Refrigerate 1 to 2 hours to set. ■

374. ■ **Choose the less-rich filling** and topping when deciding on the pie you'll make. *Vitality* magazine reported that having pecan pie with whipped cream costs 32 fat grams and 460 calories more per slice than apple pie, which gets its à la mode status from low-fat frozen yogurt. (Used by permission from *Vitality*, Dallas, Texas.)

375. ■ **Or make a fat-free crust.** The one I keep hearing about from nearly all the low-fat cooks I know is a crumb crust made by combining $1/4$ cup of thawed apple juice concentrate with 1 cup of Grape-Nuts cereal. (Depending on the consistency you want, the cereal can be blended, crushed, or left whole.) Press the cereal-juice mixture into a 9-inch pie pan. If you're using the crust for a pie that requires no baking, bake the crust for 10 minutes and then cool before filling.

376. ■ **Another nonfat piecrust** comes from George Mateljan's *Cooking Without Fat.* This one is based on fat-free cookies such as Health Valley's Date Delight or Raisin Oatmeal cookies. Process the cookies into uniform crumbs in a blender or food processor. Then press the crumbs into the pie pan with your damp fingers. For a full crust covering the bottom and sides of an 8- or 9-inch pie plate, you'll need $1 3/4$ cups of cookie crumbs (that's one package or less). If possible, chill the crust-lined pan while you prepare the filling. Even a short time in the refrigerator will improve the way the crust holds together.

When the filling will not be cooked inside the crust, bake the empty crust for about 8 minutes at 375 degrees, or until it just begins to darken. For pies with fillings that bake inside the crust, prebaking is not necessary, but partial baking (4 to 5 minutes) makes the final result crispier.

377. ■ **Or make a crisp instead of a pie.** You can expect to save at least 10 grams of fat when you choose apple crisp over standard apple pie. This delicately sweet crisp comes from the *No Salt, No Sugar, No Fat Cookbook,* by Jacqueline B. Williams with Goldie Silverman:

■ APPLE CRISP ■

Crust

> 1 cup rolled oats
> 1 cup whole wheat flour
> $1/2$ cup Grape-Nuts cereal
> 1 teaspoon cinnamon
> 1 cup unsweetened apple juice

Filling

> 2 cups sliced apples
> $1/2$ cup raisins
> 1 cup unsweetened apple juice
> 1 to 2 teaspoons cinnamon
> 1 tablespoon lemon juice
> 2 teaspoons cornstarch or arrowroot

To make crust: Preheat oven to 350 degrees. Combine dry ingredients. Stir in apple juice until mixture holds together. Press half of mixture in bottom and up sides of a nonstick 9-inch pie pan. Bake for 5 minutes. Save remaining crust for topping. To make filling: Turn up oven to 375 degrees. Combine all ingredients in a medium-size saucepan. Bring to a boil and simmer for about 10 minutes, until apples are only slightly tender. Remove apples and raisins with a slotted spoon and place in pie shell. Increase heat and continue cooking sauce until it thickens. Pour sauce over apples and raisins. Crumble remaining crust over filling. Bake for 30 minutes. *Serves 6 to 8.* ■

378. ▪ **Meringue is naturally low in fat** since it's based on egg whites. If you prefer to avoid eggs altogether (particularly raw eggs because of the possibility of salmonella contamination), the flax-seed egg substitute from chapter 2 (tip 92) can be used in meringues.

379. ▪ **Chocolate is high in fat, but the fat is in the cocoa butter,** not the cocoa powder. Therefore, cocoa powder can be used to create low-fat desserts as long as the other ingredients used are low in fat, too, as in this chocolate pudding from Debra Wasserman's *Simply Vegan: Quick Vegetarian Meals:*

▪ CHOCOLATE PUDDING ▪

$1^1/_2$ cups soy milk (I use low-fat soy milk)
3 tablespoons cornstarch
$^1/_4$ teaspoon vanilla
$^1/_4$ cup maple syrup
$^1/_4$ cup cocoa powder
2 bananas, sliced (optional)

Whisk together all ingredients except the bananas in a pot. Cook over medium heat, stirring constantly until pudding thickens. Remove pot from stove. Stir in sliced bananas if desired. Chill for at least 15 minutes before serving. *Serves 3.* ▪

380. ▪ **A top-notch-lunch box dessert** is Dream Pudding from Imagine Foods. Containing no fat whatsoever and no refined sugar, these delectable puddings come in an alphabet of flavors such as almond, butterscotch, and of course chocolate. They're packaged in individual serving sizes and found in natural foods stores.

381. ▪ **Eliminate cream cheese or eggs in cheesecake, custard, and mousse** by using soft tofu instead. Kathryn Arnold, food editor of *Delicious!* magazine, suggests doubling the spices and flavorings called for when you use tofu in these desserts. *Mod.*

An excellent recipe demonstrating this tip was contributed by cookbook author Jennifer Raymond to Dr. Neal Barnard's *Food for Life: How the New Four Food Groups Can Save Your Life:*

■ TOFU "CHEESECAKE" ■

This smooth and velvety "cheesecake" is delicious topped with a simple lemon glaze or fresh fruit. Agar flakes, which are derived from seaweed (see tip 354 on fruit gels), are used as a thickener. Look for them at your health food store.

Filling

2 tablespoons agar flakes
$2/3$ cup soy milk (I use low-fat soy milk)
$1/2$ cup raw sugar or other sweetener
$1/2$ teaspoon salt
2 teaspoons grated lemon rind
4 tablespoons lemon juice
2 teaspoons vanilla extract
1 pound tofu
1 prebaked 9-inch crumb or fat-free crust (Grape-Nuts, tip 375, or other)

Lemon Glaze

$1/3$ cup raw sugar or other sweetener
$1^1/2$ tablespoons cornstarch or arrowroot
$1^1/2$ tablespoons lemon juice
$1/2$ teaspoon grated lemon rind
$1/3$ cup water

In a saucepan, combine agar and soy milk and let stand 5 minutes. Add sugar and salt, and simmer over low heat, stirring often, for 5 minutes. Pour into a blender, add remaining filling ingredients, and blend until smooth. Smooth evenly in crust and chill for 30 minutes.

In a small saucepan, combine all glaze ingredients and whisk until smooth. Heat, stirring constantly, until mixture thickens. Allow to cool slightly, then spread over cheesecake. Chill an additional 2 hours. ▪

(Note: By increasing the amount of water in the lemon glaze recipe to one cup, you can use it to make a lemon sauce for brownies, cakes, fruits, or other desserts.)

COOKIES AND CAKES

382. ▪ **Fat-free cookies are available** at both grocery and natural foods stores. If you don't like the first package you try, select another type next time. Companies making fat-free cookies that I've enjoyed include Auburn Farms, R. W. Frookie, and Health Valley. Gingersnaps and fig bars have always been lower-fat cookie choices, and now Nabisco makes Fat Free Fig Newtons and a host of Newtons made from other fruits, too—yum.

383. ▪ **Or get the soul satisfaction of baking cookies** in your own kitchen. These cookies from *Just No Fat* by Norman Rose are easy to make and always turn out moist and chewy because of their surprise ingredient—cooked barley:

▪ ▪ ▪

▪ BROWN SUGAR–RAISIN COOKIES ▪

2¼ cups whole wheat flour (I recommend whole wheat
    pastry flour)
1½ cups light brown sugar
3 teaspoons baking powder
1 teaspoon salt
1 cup raisins
1 cup whole-grain barley, cooked and drained
1 cup nonfat skim milk (I use low-fat soy milk or Rice
    Dream)

Preheat oven to 375 degrees.

Combine and mix thoroughly the flour, sugar, baking powder, and salt. Add raisins, barley, and milk. Spoon onto a cookie sheet and bake for 8 to 10 minutes. ▪

384. ▪ **This sophisticated cookie recipe** that combines the sweetness of chocolate or carob with tart cranberries shows how using modest amounts of high-fat foods (walnuts, chocolate or carob chips, and oil or Spectrum Naturals Spread) can give richness to a special-occasion recipe while keeping the total fat content within reason. It was created by young culinary student Sonnet Pierce. (The first time I tasted these cookies, Sonnet had baked them outdoors in a solar oven she had built herself.) *Mod.*

▪ CHOCOLATE CHIP COOKIES ▪

Dry ingredients

    3 cups whole wheat pastry flour
    2 tablespoons coarsely chopped walnuts
    ½ cup chocolate or carob chips
    ¼ teaspoon salt

1 teaspoon baking powder
$^1/_2$ cup brown sugar
2 tablespoons nonfat dry milk powder or soy milk powder

Wet ingredients

$1^1/_2$ cups cranberries
$^1/_2$ cup honey
2 tablespoons Spectrum Naturals Spread or $1^1/_2$
     tablespoons light-flavored oil
2 tablespoons applesauce
$^1/_2$ cup orange juice

Preheat oven to 325 degrees. Mix dry ingredients together. Fold cranberries into dry ingredients. Cream together honey and Spectrum Naturals Spread. Then beat applesauce and orange juice into the honey mixture. Stir wet and dry ingredients together; the mixture will be somewhat crumbly. Shape into cookies with your hands. Bake for 15 to 20 minutes, or until bottoms are golden. *Makes 20 large cookies.* ■

385. ■ **Since bananas can fill in for both oil and eggs** as suggested in tips 358 and 366, banana cookies are naturals for this style of baking. This final cookie recipe (okay, I admit it, I like cookies) comes from *Simply Good: Recipes & More* from the Center for Conservative Therapy:

■ BANANA-DATE COOKIES ■

$1^1/_2$ cups pitted dates
2 cups water
4 cups rolled oats, finely ground
$^1/_4$ teaspoon baking soda
1 teaspoon baking powder
1 teaspoon cinnamon

$^1/_2$ teaspoon nutmeg
4 (ripe) bananas
Additional rolled oats—just enough to sprinkle over
    cookie sheet

Preheat oven to 375 degrees.

In a small saucepan, combine the dates and water. Simmer for 30 minutes. Then remove from heat. Combine all the dry ingredients, mix well, and set aside. Let the dates cool. Mash the bananas but leave them chunky. When the dates are completely cooled, combine all the ingredients and mix them until all the dry ingredients are just moistened. Be sure not to overmix the dough.

Sprinkle the cookie sheet with rolled oats. Place the dough, 1 tablespoon at a time, onto the prepared cookie sheet. Bake for 8 to 10 minutes. The cookies will be moist when they are done. ▪

386. ▪ **Sometimes the best dessert is only slightly sweet,** a delicate close to a meal or a pleasant little something with conversation and a mug of hot coffee or fragrant tea. This oil-free gingerbread from Jennifer Raymond's *The Peaceful Palate* is my favorite not-too-sweet finale to dinners both simple and grand.

▪ **GINGERBREAD** ▪

$^1/_2$ cup raisins
$^1/_2$ cup pitted dates, chopped
$1^3/_4$ cups water
$^3/_4$ cup raw sugar or other sweetener
$^1/_2$ teaspoon salt
2 teaspoons cinnamon
1 teaspoon ginger
$^3/_4$ teaspoon nutmeg

$^1/_4$ teaspoon cloves

2 cups flour (Jennifer recommends whole wheat pastry flour)

1 teaspoon baking soda

1 teaspoon baking powder

Preheat oven to 350 degrees.

Combine dried fruits, water, sugar, and seasonings in a large saucepan and bring to a boil. Continue boiling for 2 minutes. Then remove from heat and cool completely. When fruit mixture is cool, mix in dry ingredients. Spread into a prepared 9 × 9-inch pan and bake for 30 minutes, or until a toothpick inserted into the center comes out clean. *Makes one 9 × 9-inch cake.* ■

This gingerbread contains no animal ingredients and no added fat, yet it is moist and delicious. Try serving it with hot applesauce for a real treat.

387. ■ **Of conventional cakes, angel food is lowest in fat.**

388. ■ **This carrot cake, moist and delicious with only 0.6 grams total fat,** comes from chef Mark Hall and appears in *Dr. Dean Ornish's Program for Reversing Heart Disease:*

■ CARROT CAKE ■

1 teaspoon ground cinnamon

1 teaspoon ground allspice

$^1/_2$ teaspoon freshly grated nutmeg

$^1/_4$ teaspoon ground cloves

$1^1/_2$ cups whole wheat pastry flour

$^1/_3$ cup wheat bran

$1^1/_2$ teaspoons baking powder

1 teaspoon baking soda

1 cup grated carrots

1 cup raisins or other dried fruit

^{3}/$_4$ cup honey

1^1/$_2$ cups water

Preheat oven to 350 degrees. Combine all the dry ingredients and mix well. In a separate bowl combine the honey and water. Fold the dry ingredients into the wet ones and mix well. Do not overbeat or mix. Pour into a nonstick 9 × 5 × 3-inch loaf pan. Bake for 1 hour and 15 minutes, or until a toothpick comes out clean. *Makes 10 slices.* ■

TOPPINGS AND FROZEN TREATS

389. ■ **If you want cream cheese frosting for your carrot cake** (or for something else you bake), look for a fat-reduced soy or dairy cream cheese, or substitute tofu for the cream cheese, or replace it with yogurt cheese made from nonfat yogurt. To make yogurt cheese, freeze yogurt, thaw, and pour into a sieve lined with cheesecloth. Set the sieve over a medium bowl and let drain for 1 hour. What's left in the sieve is your yogurt cheese. (This does not work well with soy yogurt, so if you want to stay away from dairy, use tofu—*mod.*—in the frosting.)

390. ■ **The raison d'être for cream toppings on desserts** is often to tone down the sweetness of the dish. If you make a less sweet dessert, you'll eliminate the need for whipped cream or a similar topping.

391. ■ **Or make whipped cream with less than one-half gram of fat per cup** by whipping chilled evaporated skim milk instead. Chill your mixing bowl and mixer, too, and serve immediately. (Evaporated skim milk can also substitute for heavy cream in recipes.)

392. ▪ **The whipped cream I serve company** is this one from *The High Road to Health,* by Lindsay Wagner and Ariane Spade:

▪ MOCK WHIPPED CREAM ▪

$^1/_2$ cup mild soy milk
$^1/_2$ teaspoon agar flakes
1 tablespoon water
2 teaspoons cold-pressed vegetable oil
$^1/_8$ teaspoon cream of tartar
1 teaspoon vanilla
1 teaspoon to 1 tablespoon honey

Mix the soy milk, agar, and water in a small saucepan and bring to boil. Simmer, covered, for 5 minutes until the agar has dissolved. Stir twice. Pour the soy milk mixture into a measuring cup and add just enough water to make $^1/_2$ cup. Refrigerate for 45 minutes.

Then combine the chilled soy milk with the oil, cream of tartar, and vanilla, and beat at high speed with an electric eggbeater. After about 3 minutes, slowly add the honey. Total whipping time is about 10 minutes. Cream will form into gentle peaks. Serve over fresh fruit or wherever you would use real whipped cream. ▪

393. ▪ **As a sweet topping for fresh fruit,** try either nonfat sour cream or soft tofu (*mod.*) with the addition of sugar or other sweetener and vanilla powder or extract.

394. ▪ **When fruit salad is your final course,** dress it up with a sprinkle of cardamom.

395. ▪ **Pureed fruits beautifully top fruit salads or plain cakes.** Start your blender or food processor with sliced, ripe bananas. (It may take a tablespoon or so of water to get the blender going.) Then add berries—strawberries, raspberries, or blueberries—for a beautiful, creamy sauce. (Using frozen berries makes a thicker sauce.) Serve immediately.

396. ▪ **Sorbets and ices are fat-free coolers** all summer long. Sherbet is also a low-fat choice.

397. ▪ **Nonfat frozen yogurt** has earned its popularity with a deceptively rich taste and wide availability. Be sure your frozen yogurt is indeed nonfat or at least very low in fat; the fat content of frozen yogurt can be zero, or as high as that of ice cream.

398. ▪ **Nondairy frozen desserts** also vary in their fat content depending upon brand and flavor. There are some wonderful choices out there. I make room in my freezer for several, including Living Lightly (as rich-tasting as premium ice cream with flavors including refreshing Mint-Carob and the purist simplicity of Vanilla with only 8 percent of calories from fat); and Sweet Nothings—nine fabulous flavors, not a touch of fat in any of them. Sweet Nothings Espresso Fudge gets raves every time I serve it.

399. ▪ **What has the consistency and sweetness of frozen custard** but is made only of fruit? Magic Banana Ice Cream, that's what! It really is magical to see bananas turn into a tempting treat for children and grown-up children alike. The best appliance I know of for making this is the Champion Juicer, sold at many health food stores. If you don't have one of these, you can use your food processor with the metal blade in place.

First, freeze peeled, very ripe bananas overnight or for as long as four days. If you'll be using a food processor, chop the bananas in two-inch lengths before freezing and freeze them on a cookie sheet or in another container so they're not touching each other. If you have a Champion Juicer, run the bananas through the juicer with the piece called the "homogenizer blank" in place. If using a processor, puree the frozen banana slices, stopping every so often to scrape the puree from the sides of the processor bowl. The "ice cream" is ready when it's velvety smooth. Allow two bananas per person for generous servings.

You can use these directions to make frozen desserts using other fruits—peaches, strawberries, mangoes, your choice—but the result will be more a sorbet and less an "ice cream" than if you use bananas. A stunning finish to a dinner party can come from layering the banana dessert with colorful sorbets made from other fruits in tall, clear compote glasses.

400. ■ **Chocolate sauce is a treasured substance** for many people, and going low fat needn't mean giving that up. A company called Wax Orchards makes fudge sauces you'd never believe were fat free and naturally sweetened to boot. Among the flavors are Classic Fudge Sweet (dark chocolate) and Oh, Fudge! (a lovely, light chocolate). Warmed gently, these can be served over frozen desserts, drizzled over fruit, or used in hot dessert beverages. Look for these in natural foods stores and gourmet shops, or order direct from Wax Orchards, 22744 Wax Orchards Road, Vashon, WA 98070.

CHAPTER 8

Get the Fat Out
When You Eat Out

I f Rip van Winkle were to wake up today, he would find that tastes have changed more in restaurant dining than perhaps anywhere else in the past twenty years. When Rip started snoozing, no self-respecting chef could have gotten along without the butter, cream, and egg yolks of traditional French cookery. When European-trained chefs came to the United States, they brought the butter and cream but adopted the American penchant for centering every meal around a large piece of meat. We ended up with the high-fat habits of two cultures every time we went out for dinner.

Now, younger, American-trained chefs are developing their own style, their own cuisine, and their own way to respond to the public's demand for lighter fare. However, because people who want to consume low-fat, high-natural carbohydrate foods are not yet seen as the majority by restaurateurs, menus rarely show the variety of low-fat and fat-free dishes that are truly available. For this reason, we'll be covering tips on both what (and what not) to order from the menu and how to order what isn't even there.

Of course, eating out often means grabbing a bite somewhere that has no menu. As most of us frequently eat at drive-throughs, diners, truck stops, street kiosks, mall food courts, and the like, it makes sense for us to know how to do our best at these bastions of grill and grease. But times are changing. The fact is, with few exceptions you can get a healthful, low-fat meal that will tide you over until the next one at virtually any restaurant—whether it's the type where you're greeted with "Good evening, monsieur and madame," or "What'll it be?"

And remember that many of the tips in the preceding sections of this book can be translated for use in dining-out situations as well. You may find yourself educating servers and chefs. A couple I know in Connecticut were fond of a particular restaurant's fried potato skins and missed them when they switched to a low-fat diet. In talking one evening with the headwaiter, they asked if it wouldn't be possible to serve something similar but without all the fat. They suggested hollowing out baked potatoes and stuffing the skins with seasoned mashed potato and an assortment of steamed vegetables rather than with bacon and cheese. The chef made this dish for them and was so pleased with the result that the next time my friends went to that restaurant, their potato creation was on the menu—named after them!

GETTING WHAT YOU WANT

401. ■ **Seek out restaurants featuring "spa," "contemporary," or "California" cuisine,** or those that have little heart symbols on their menus. This means that the selections, or at least a portion of them, are designed to be lower in fat (and often lower in salt) than standard fare.

402. ▪ **Natural foods restaurants can offer an array of choices,** but seldom are they all low in fat. As in any other restaurant, concentrate on vegetables, fruits, whole grains, and legumes that haven't been fried or defiled with oily extras.

403. ▪ **Call ahead when you can.** Restaurants are in business to please their customers. It's in their best interest to provide you with what you want. Even so, they can't work miracles. If someone shows up at seven P.M., the kitchen staff can only accommodate a special request from what they have on hand. If they receive a call in the morning with that request, however, restaurant people will usually go out of their way to oblige.

▪ BONUS TIP: *Be sure to remember an accommodating server when it comes time to tip. Meatless entrees are the least expensive ones on the menu, so if you order these and say no to cocktails and dessert as well, your server ends up with 15 percent of not very much. A bit of extra generosity would be appreciated.*

404. ▪ **Mix and match from the menu.** As long as the food is on hand, you can get it, in spite of what it's teamed with on the menu. A physician I once interviewed has a favorite restaurant that covers poached pears with *crème anglaise* (made from egg yolks—pure cholesterol). However, their chocolate mousse (heavy saturated fat) gets a healthful raspberry sauce. The doctor responds by ordering his own innovation: *les poires aux framboises*—the pears with the raspberry sauce. *Voilà!* Sweet elegance and no fat.

405. ▪ **Communicate clearly with your server,** in hopes that he or she will communicate clearly with the kitchen. Repeating your request more than once is a good idea: "Let me be sure I was clear about this. I want the Caesar salad with lemon wedges instead of Caesar dressing and my entree needs to be cooked without any butter or oil."

406. ▪ **Put it in writing.** If you have a medical condition that makes sticking to a low-fat diet imperative, if you're a committed vegetarian, or if you're simply someone who wants what you want with no surprises, it's frustrating to know the high probability that your lucid explanation may not reach the cook as stated. The reason is that servers and chefs seldom *talk* to each other. The people in the kitchen get their information from what's written on the ticket.

But you can communicate directly with the chef via those little return address labels you can order cheaply through the mail. They can say anything you want them to: "Please use no butter, oil, egg yolks, whole milk, or cheese on this order. Thank you," or "No meat, no fish, no eggs, no oil, no dairy, no kidding. Thanks." Give one to your server to stick on the ticket along with your order.

This may seem like an extreme measure, but for those who are weary of being told, "Chicken isn't meat" or "Parmesan isn't cheese," it's a godsend. It also takes the pressure off busy wait-people. (This doesn't work in those restaurants in which orders get to the kitchen via computer. Perhaps one day there will be a no-fat command in restaurant software.)

407. ▪ Be willing to ask questions, regardless of what the menu says. Once while traveling, I stayed at a hotel whose menu boasted a "light" section that was supposedly overseen by a dietitian. The breakfast cereal choices were oatmeal and granola. I assumed (big mistake, assuming) that meant oil-free granola, but what arrived was a high-fat commercial brand, laden with oil and full of coconut. I'd been lulled by the menu's assurance that someone was looking out for me. Wrong. I have to look out for myself.

408. ▪ Bargain at restaurants to save fat the way you'd bargain at a garage sale to save money. If, for example, you want a vegetable plate and the waitperson tells you there isn't one, ask, "What comes with the rack of lamb?" (or the roast beef or the fried chicken). If it's a nice restaurant, the server will probably say something like, "A salad of tossed young greens, rice pilaf or a baked potato, steamed broccoli, and sourdough rolls." Then you can say, "Fine, I'll have the rack of lamb—hold the lamb—and bring me both the rice and the potato." (When side dishes are listed on the menu, you can order several and make a meal that way.)

409. ■ **Don't expect financial compensation** when you choose to eliminate certain parts of full dinners, even though you're saving the restaurant a bundle on all the rich, expensive food you're not eating. A friend of mine is a regular at a particular restaurant where she likes to get taco salad without the beef, cheese, or sour cream. If she asks for so much as an extra bean, however, there is a surcharge on the bill. The major exception to this is buffet-style dining. If you let the management at a smorgasbord restaurant know you'll be eating meatless that meal, they'll almost always give you a deal.

MENU SAVVY

410. ■ **Most appetizers are purposely high in fat** and salt to awaken your taste buds, and tease your appetite. But if you come to dinner hungry, your appetite will do just fine on its own. When you do want a starter, choose:

411. ■ **Fresh fruit or juice.**

412. ■ **Or tomato juice** (add a little Tabasco or Worcestershire sauce).

413. ■ **Or salad with lemon wedges** or an oil-free dressing.

414. ■ **Or gazpacho.**

415. ■ **Or crudités** (replace a high-fat dip with nonfat yogurt, salsa, cocktail sauce, oil-free salad dressing—whatever you can negotiate).

416. ▪ **And ask for your salad minus unwanted garnishes**—cheese, egg, olives, bacon bits, croutons.

417. ▪ **Order salad dressing on the side** and just dip the edge of each forkful into the dressing. It's amazing how little dressing it takes to give greens a rich taste. *Mod.*

418. ▪ **You can make your own low-fat salad dressing** right at your table by asking for some Dijon mustard and balsamic vinegar (or, in a pinch, whatever mustard and vinegar you can get).

419. ▪ **If you frequent salad bars** (or if you're a big salad eater whether there's a bar or not), you may want to bring your own oil-free dressing or seasoned rice vinegar with you. (I pack mine in 2-ounce watertight containers called Midgets, available from any Tupperware consultant.)

420. ▪ **Having soup?** Go for clear instead of cream soup. (If you want a vegetable broth base, you may be out of luck, although some accommodating restaurants will make you a soup separate from the communal pot.)

421. ▪ **An easy way to cut the fat** when you eat out is to ask for the dish you want to be served without sauce. Restaurant sauces can add a lot of fat without an equal return in satiety.

422. ▪ **Ask that whatever you're ordering be prepared without oil.** (After some time of cooking at home with minimal oil, it's easy to forget how much of it other people can use.)

423. ▪ **If what you want appears on the menu as a fried selection,** ask if you can have it steamed or broiled instead. And don't be deceived by phrases like "cholesterol free" and "cooked in all-natural vegetable oil." Deep-fried is deep-fried and you're worth better.

424. ▪ **If you still insist on a steak dinner every now**

and then, the leaner cuts are filet mignon, London broil, round steak, and flank steak with the visible fat removed. Order the smallest steak you can or share one with your dining partner. Fill up on the salad, vegetables, rice, potato, and bread. *Inter.*

425. ▪ **Always choose rice or a baked potato over french fries.** Bypass the sour cream for your potato, but keep the chives. Steak sauce is another restaurant potato topping, as are salsa, ketchup, mustard, and hot sauce. Even a little olive oil (*mod.*) is a better choice than butter or margarine. (See the potato-topping tips in chapter 5 for more ideas.)

426. ▪ **If the dessert is to die for** but longevity is appealing, too, split the delicacy with your dinner partner. It doesn't take much of a rich dessert to satisfy the craving for a sweet finish, and if you're out with a date or mate, two forks and one pastry are quite romantic. *Mod.*

INTERNATIONAL INSIGHTS

427. ▪ **Frequent ethnic eateries.** Not all the food there is low in fat, but you can find entrees that rely less on meat, more on grains and vegetables. You can negotiate about sauces and cooking methods. The array of international cuisine that can be found in big cities—and many small ones as well—is staggering. Included here are ten of the most widely available:

428. ▪ **When the restaurant is French,** look for the simplest selections. Start with a green salad or, if you eat fish, *salade niçoise* (dressing eliminated or on the side). Go with wine-based sauces instead of creamy ones, and the lighter dishes such as bouillabaisse (*inter.*) or ratatouille.

429. ▪ **Chinese restaurants can steam what is usually stir-fried** or stir-fry with minimal oil if requested. They can also bring you crunchy spring rolls in rice paper wrappers instead of fried egg rolls. Look for vegetable dishes and avoid fried rice, meat, and appetizers, oily Sichuan dishes, egg foo yung, and lobster sauce. Bean curd (*mod.*) can be substituted for meat in almost any dish.

430. ▪ **Japanese restaurants provide adventures in low-fat dining** when you avoid the fried dishes you can recognize with the words "tempura" and "agemono." Concentrate on rice, soba noodles, miso soup, and sushi. Sukiyaki is a classic Japanese dish of vegetables and thinly sliced beef (*inter.*) or tofu (*mod.*) cooked in soy sauce, rice wine, sugar, and water, prepared at the table. Traditionally, a bite of rice is eaten with every bite of sukiyaki, keeping the fat of the total meal even lower.

431. ▪ **Vietnamese eateries are superb** for—literally—dining to your heart's content. Since most Vietnamese restaurants in the United States are family owned and fairly small, you can have a lot of input into exactly what is prepared for you. At the one near my house, I've often been invited into the kitchen to show the owner (who is also the chef) what I want. Every dish is replete with lightly cooked vegetables and many contain delicious rice noodles.

▪ BONUS TIP: *Cilantro, a common flavoring in Vietnamese cuisine, is a pungent relative of ordinary parsley. It's said that 90 percent of people like cilantro a lot, but to the other 10 percent it tastes like soap. If you're new to cilantro, try some separately before committing yourself to a dish that's full of it.*

432. ▪ **Indian places are great choices** for anyone who appreciates powerful spices, heady curries, and an abundance of meatless entrees. Stay away from the fried breads and fried appetizers and communicate as best you can your desire to avoid *ghee,* the clarified butter that goes into almost everything.

433. ▪ **Ethiopian restaurants are worth looking for when you travel** if you don't live in a major city that has one or more of them. Since forks are regarded as weapons in Ethiopia, they are not used. Instead food is served from a large common platter in the center of the table and diners wrap each portion they take in a piece of *injera,* a delectable, crepelike bread.

It is customary in Ethiopian cuisine to use large quantities of oil, but having prepared this food myself I know it can be done with much, much less. Make it clear that you want little or no oil used and make your selection from *yekik we't* (a split pea sauce traditionally prepared with onions, wine, and red pepper), *azifa* (green lentils with spices), or *ye'atakilt alich'a* (vegetable stew with onions, potatoes, and carrots).

434. ▪ **In the mood for Greek food?** The salad appetizer *tzatzaki,* the fish dish *plaki* (*inter.*), and the garlicky potato dip *skordalia* should be low in fat. So is Greek salad if the feta cheese and olives are held and you ask for the dressing (*mod.*) on the side. Pita bread is a filling accompaniment. *Dolmas*— stuffed grape leaves—can always be ordered with rice instead of lamb. Phyllo pastries are avoided by the prudent.

435. ▪ **Middle Eastern restaurants provide ample selections** including tabouli (ask to have it with no extra oil), couscous, rice pilaf, and small amounts of hummus (*mod.*) spread on lots of pita bread.

436. ▪ **Italian places are among the easiest of all** to leave feeling full but not fat. Eschew cream sauces on your pasta in favor of those based on tomato or wine, and ask for the olive oil to be left out. Another low-fat option is gnocchi, a traditional potato dumpling; order it with oil-free marinara sauce.

You can get pizza with half the regular amount of cheese (*mod.*) or, better still, no cheese at all. Let the restaurant know you want no skimping on the tomato sauce and lots of low-fat toppings—peppers, tomatoes, mushrooms, onion, garlic, broccoli, spinach, and (although I've never quite understood this one) pineapple.

■ B O N U S   T I P : *If you're ordering a cheeseless pizza to carry out, open the box to be sure of what you're getting. A couple of times I've ended up with a pizza that had cheese but no sauce.*

437. ■ **Mexican restaurants can be challenging.** Committed low-fat diners have been known to order double portions of the leanest choices—Spanish rice and corn or flour tortillas with a plethora of lettuce, onions, and tomatoes. Burritos or soft tacos are preferred to crispy (fried) tacos. If you choose a meat filling (*inter.*) you may want to forgo the cheese, or vice versa.

I sometimes get a cheeseless bean burrito (*mod.*) with extra vegetables, although I am aware that the beans are almost invariably fried. If lard is used, I skip the beans and have a guacamole burrito (*mod.*). Guacamole is high in fat, too, but it's a legitimate exception in a low-fat lifestyle.

Of course, it's a good idea to pass over those chips on the table (even though they're free). One of my friends brings non-fat tortilla chips (Guiltless Gourmet is her brand) so she can enjoy the hot sauce grease free.

ON THE RUN
AND ON THE ROAD

438. ■ **Instead of eating fast food twice a week,** go out once a week to a place that's really nice. You deserve a relaxing meal with linen napkins and somebody else to clear the table. You'll also be more likely to get low-fat food at restaurants that keep a slower pace.

439. ▪ **All fast food shouldn't be lumped together** as nutritionally inferior, however. Some of it is actually quite good. Select the places offering salad, baked potatoes, à la carte vegetables, food bars with pasta and veggies, or specialties they'll make for you in a fat-reduced version.

440. ▪ **If you yearn for a hamburger** (*inter.*), get a plain one with mustard or ketchup and vegetables instead of a double burger or one with additions like bacon, mayonnaise, or cheese.

441. Or . . . satisfy a burger craving with a veggie burger. As of this writing, at least one major fast-food chain is test-marketing such an alternative burger. Some of the more formal restaurant chains including T.G.I. Friday's and the Hard Rock Cafe (as well as such unanticipated spots as the Smithsonian Air & Space Museum and Yosemite National Park) serve the "gardenburger." Developed by Wholesome & Hearty Foods, Inc., of Portland, Oregon, the gardenburger contains fresh mushrooms, onions, brown rice, low-fat cheeses, oats, and spices, and keeps its calories from fat to a respectable 18.5 percent.

442. ▪ **Beware of fast-food chicken and fish sandwiches.** They're likely to be fried and have more fat than a regular hamburger.

443. ▪ **Remember the vegetable sandwiches from chapter 6?** Use that information to help out when you find yourself hungry in a burger-and-fries place and would rather not indulge in the expected fare. Some of the burger purveyors are happy to make you their biggest sandwich-on-a-bun with vegetables only: lettuce, tomatoes, pickle, and onion can, in enough quantity and accompanied by mustard and ketchup, make a decent sandwich. If you're still hungry, have two of them. In nosheries with salad bars, you can ask for a couple of buns when you place your order and make your own sandwiches.

444. ▪ **Sub shops are super.** The choice lowest in fat is a veggie sub without cheese, mayonnaise, olives, or oil. Instead go for lettuce, tomato, green peppers, jalapeños, sprouts, pickle, onion, a squirt of spicy mustard, and a splash of vinegar.

445. ▪ **Out for breakfast?** Look for oatmeal, cream of wheat, dry cereal, toast, bagels, English muffins, low-fat muffins, cantaloupe, grapefruit, stewed prunes, and fresh juices. Use jam instead of butter, juice or nonfat milk instead of whole milk. (Refer to chapter 2. Some of its at-home suggestions can be applied to restaurant breakfasts, too.)

▪ BONUS TIP: *Take the time to fill out the customer opinion forms provided by many chain restaurants, or use their toll-free customer service numbers. Thank them for the low-fat food they already offer and let them know what else you'd like to see. Tell the restaurant managers, too. Individual franchisees, when enough of their patrons comment on something, can have a major impact on corporate policy.*

446. ▪ **Staying low fat while traveling by car can be a challenge,** so review all the basic eating-out tips when you're going to be on the road. Look for familiar chains that you know to have suitable sandwiches or better-than-average salad bars. You may also want to pack some snacks from home since fresh fruit, good salads, and low-fat entrees can be in short supply at highway restaurants. On long trips, I find it worth the extra time to get off the interstate at least once a day for a leisurely meal in town.

447. ▪ **If you're flying, order a special meal.** These need to be requested when you reserve your ticket and it's a good idea to reconfirm your special meal twenty-four hours before the flight. The special meals are just like other airline food, seldom anything to write home about unless you're in First Class.

Most airlines have choices including "low fat," "low cholesterol," "lacto-vegetarian," and "pure vegetarian." Once I'd ordered pure vegetarian and the man next to me had ordered low cholesterol. When he saw what I was served, he complained to the flight attendant that my food had less cholesterol (none, in fact) than his. (And the curried rice dish I got looked quite a bit more appetizing than his skinless chicken fillet.)

448. ▪ **There's always popcorn at carnivals,** festivals, amusement parks, exhibitions, outdoor concerts, sporting events, and fairs. It's not air-popped, but even oil-popped corn (*mod.*) is a better-than-average pick for an away-from-home snack. Other offerings you can count on at such events (in addition to the crowds and spending more than you'd planned to) are:

449. ▪ **Soft pretzels.**

450. ▪ **Giant pickles.**

451. ▪ **Snow cones** (also known as shaved ice), Popsicles, and frozen bananas.

452. ▪ **Frosty lemonade** and nonalcoholic piña coladas so thick with crushed ice they can be eaten with a spoon.

453. ▪ **Nonfat frozen yogurt** and sometimes creamy, low-fat, nondairy frozen treats as well.

454. ▪ **Candied apples** (the cinnamon ones are lower in fat than the caramel and they won't be rolled in crushed peanuts).

455. ▪ **And corn on the cob.** It's great—just get it before it's been drenched with melted butter.

CHAPTER 9

Get the Fat Off Your Body
and Out of Your Life

I f people change their diet but everything else in their lives remains the same, I wouldn't bet any money on the durability of their dietary change. Altering behavior without altering attitude is seldom productive. That's particularly applicable here since living lean involves not only low-fat food choices but a new outlook, as well as dedication to exercise, self-care, and healthful living.

Dr. Dean Ornish's well-known program for reversing coronary heart disease is not just a dietary regimen. In addition to meatless meals that keep fat intake to 10 percent of calories, the Ornish approach involves moderate exercise, yoga, stress management, and peer support. Such a multifaceted strategy is ideal for getting the fat out of people's lives, whether the fat is arterial, abdominal, or attitudinal.

There is more to a human being than a digestive system. Getting the fat out is not "going on a diet." Diets are temporary, self-defeating, and depressing. Getting the fat out is making a commitment to be more open to life. It's saying, "I plan to be around a good, long time, and I'm worth taking care of." This is an empowering prospect.

That is not to say that changing one's lifestyle is ever without challenge. We have to revamp habits that we've had so long we can hardly tell where they stop and we start. Exercise, even if it's a brief daily walk, can sometimes loom before us as a major undertaking instead of a twenty-minute outing. And as we make these changes we're living in the real world with families, friends, and coworkers—some of whom would rather see us in front of the TV munching nachos than putting bean soup in the slow-cooker and going out for a bike ride.

This final chapter discusses such pragmatic matters as these. It also touches on those aspects of getting the fat out that relate to how you look as well as to how you cook. Your body may never reach some overblown standard of perfection set by the media. Nevertheless, eating low-fat, high-complex carbohydrate foods and getting regular physical activity will guarantee that you'll be in the best shape possible for you. And that's important—so you can do your work, love your family, enjoy your friends, and make your mark on this world.

GETTING STARTED

456. ■ **If you're under a doctor's care, stay in close touch** with him or her as you make your dietary changes. Dosages of certain medications (including those for high cholesterol, high blood pressure, and diabetes) often need to be modified as a result of markedly decreasing dietary fat and cholesterol.

457. ■ **Set your fat intake goal low enough** that you'll be rewarded for your efforts. Although most health organizations in this country suggest getting fat to under 30 percent of calories, much solid evidence suggests that this may be a too liberal maximum. Educate yourself and discuss your findings with your doctor. (Be aware that becoming an M.D. does not mean a physician is no longer an H.B.—human being. Many doctors eat high-fat diets and are reluctant to advise their patients to do something they themselves do not.)

■ BONUS TIP: *For nutritional counseling your doctor may not have the time or the specialized training to provide, seek out a registered dietitian. To locate one near you, call the American Dietetic Association (800-366-1655). If you're interested in a meatless diet, look for a member of Vegetarian Nutrition, a dietetic practice group of the ADA.*

An independent resource for health professionals desiring more nutritional knowledge is the Institute of Nutrition Education, 1601 N. Sepulveda Boulevard, #342, Manhattan Beach, CA 90266.

458. ■ **Eliminate first the fats that are most expendable:** butter on vegetables, oily dressing on salads, the fried version of a food just as easily baked or steamed.

459. ■ **Eradicate from your kitchen** those foods, utensils, and cookbooks that do not support your conviction to get the fat out. You can have a profitable tag sale as a result of this and use the proceeds for a pressure cooker, a nonstick wok, a vegetable juicer—whatever it takes to make cutting fat easier than eating it.

460. ■ **When you're not the cook** and you question whether or not a food is high in fat, surreptitiously blot it with your napkin. A smear indicates a fatty food.

461. ■ **Learn to decipher food labels,** particularly as they apply to fat. The fat content and nutritional status of prepared and packaged foods range from appalling to excellent. In standardizing portion sizes, defining terms such as "low cholesterol" and "fat free," and limiting health claims manufacturers can make on a product to those with credible scientific backup, the

1994 U.S. labeling requirements represent a tremendous improvement over previous labels.

Nevertheless, for some mysterious reason they fail to give the percentage of calories from fat. You can figure that yourself by dividing the calories from fat per serving (listed on the label) by the total calories per serving (also on the label) and multiplying your answer by 100.

If you are not fond of math, know that foods labeled "low fat" have 3 grams of fat or less per 100-calorie serving (entrees and some dairy products are exemptions from this), and foods labeled "fat free" must have less than 0.5 gram of fat per serving.

462. ■ **If you're most comfortable keeping a numeric count** of the amount of fat you ingest, get yourself a clear, easy-to-follow fat gram counter and familiarize yourself with it. One that I like is *The Fat & Cholesterol Counter* from the American Heart Association. It fits in a pocket.

■ BONUS TIP: *You can figure the grams of fat you want to eat in a day based on the number of calories you consume. If you eat 1,500 calories a day and want your diet to be below 30 percent of calories from fat, your fat intake maximum would be 50 grams per day. If you want no more than 15 percent of your calories to come from fat, consume no more than 25 grams of fat each day. Of course, if you center your diet on vegetables, grains, legumes, and fruit with the bare minimum of added oil, your fat intake will stay this low without having to count anything.*

463. ■ **It's smart to plan low-fat meals in advance** and have the necessary ingredients on hand. The idea is to make the establishment of new habits as effortless as possible, and make reverting to old habits difficult.

464. ■ **Explore interesting venues for your food shopping.** In addition to the supermarket and natural foods store, go to farmers' markets and roadside produce stands, "pick-your-own" orchards, gourmet shops, and international markets. Even midsize cities often have Indian, West African, Chinese, Japanese, Korean, Vietnamese, kosher, Mexican, Italian, and Middle Eastern food stores.

465. ▪ **Grow a garden.** Or at least grow something, if it's only a potted tomato plant on your balcony or fresh herbs on a kitchen windowsill. The healthiest people I know are gardeners. That's partly because for some months every year they're forced to eat vast quantities of vitamin-rich, low-fat vegetables since they have so many of them. But there's another aspect: it's healing to the body and soul to dig in the dirt and get friendly with Mother Nature one on one.

466. ▪ **Another way to obtain natural, low-fat foods inexpensively** is to join with others and get your food directly from the grower or producer. If you hook up with a community-supported agriculture (CSA) group, you become a shareholder for a growing season in an organic farm. Every week you get a bag of just-picked produce from "your farm." And food co-ops or private buying clubs make it possible to buy staples and packaged foods at a substantial discount.

467. ▪ **Eat simple meals and incorporate other time-saving practices** into your food preparation. Among them:

468. ▪ **Plan a week of menus** and shop just once for everything.

469. ▪ **Keep frozen vegetables on hand.**

470. ▪ **Use a Crockpot** to let soups and stews cook while you're away.

471. ▪ **Prepare soup in quantity.** If you can't eat it all within a few days, freeze what's left in ice-cube trays and thaw as many soup cubes as you need for a quick lunch.

472. ▪ **Make rice and beans in advance** and keep canned beans in your cupboards (see tip 237) for use throughout the week in a variety of recipes. (Remember that cold rice can be quickly reheated in a microwave or by steaming.)

473. ■ **Incorporate leftovers into your meals.** Steamed vegetables can be marinated for salads, used in sauces, or tossed into stir-fries just long enough to heat them through. Cooked grains and potatoes can be recycled into soups or rolled in cabbage leaves, collard greens, or grape leaves. Sunday night's fruit salad can go into Monday morning's smoothie.

■ BONUS TIP: *Know enough about your protein needs to avoid being deceived. People justify eating outrageous amounts of fat with, "Well, I figured I needed the protein." That's like a wino saying he needs to get iron from the grapes! Protein often fraternizes with fat (as in meats, cheeses, peanut butter). See that most of yours keeps better company.*

Since there is protein in virtually every natural food, no varied, calorie-sufficient, whole foods diet will be deficient in it. And you don't need to do any complicated combinations of grains and beans to get the protein you need; just base each meal around a satisfying starch and set it off with vegetables and fruits.

474. ■ **Give yourself the advantage of consistency,** enabling your tastes to change so that low-fat foods will be not only the right choice but your first choice. Research done at the Monell Chemical Senses Center in Philadelphia suggests that cutting out high-fat foods leads to a preference for those low in fat; even consumption of the laboratory-formulated "phony fats" can impede this.

475. ■ **If you are going to "cheat" on occasion, cheat productively.** In other words, do your fudging on a piece of Grandma's fudge (which is undeniably out of this world) instead of on a cello-wrapped grocery-store rendition not nearly good enough to justify its fat and sugar content.

THE ACTIVE INGREDIENT

476. ■ **The right kind of exercise burns fat** and strengthens your heart and respiratory system. It is *aerobic,* but not necessarily *aerobics.* It is any exercise that moderately elevates your heart rate and keeps it there for at least 15 minutes. (Twenty minutes is the usual recommendation because it takes the body time to reach its aerobic heart rate level.) The way to get this kind of exercise is to use the big muscles of your lower body—thighs and buttocks—in activities such as walking, jogging, biking, and dancing.

■ BONUS TIP: *There are lots of good books about exercise. My favorite is* The New Fit or Fat *by Covert Bailey. I read it while I walked on the treadmill.*

477. ■ **Figure your aerobic target zone** and exercise at that level. You can get a pretty good idea that you're exercising within your aerobic range if you can carry on a comfortable conversation while you work out. You can also take your pulse from time to time during exercise or invest in a heart rate monitor.

There are formulas you can use to calculate how rapidly your heart should beat for your exercise to qualify as aerobic. One easy way to get a fairly accurate idea of your training heart rate is to subtract your age from 180. Exercise within a ten-beat range with the resulting number at the top. (For example, let's say you're thirty years old: 180 minus 30 is 150, so your target heart range would be 140 to 150.)

478. ■ **If you want to exercise more, go for time, not intensity.** Everyone should exercise aerobically at least three times a week. Most healthy people can beneficially engage in aerobic exercise six days a week. Postexercise muscle repair does take longer in people over forty, making variety (such as walking one day, swimming the next) an especially good idea. Although you can exercise as long as you like, exercising hard enough to go beyond your target heart rate puts you outside aerobic parameters. Then your body is being fueled by glycogen, not fat.

This was brought home to me when I asked an aerobics instructor why she and her colleagues took aerobics classes in addition to teaching them. "When we teach," she said, "we work so hard shouting and keeping the pace for everybody else, we're not working aerobically. If we didn't take other classes, we'd add fat." (The fact is, many aerobics classes are too intense for the average person and therefore not aerobic at all. If you're in a class, check your pulse periodically and slow down if you need to.)

479. ■ **Learn the auxiliary perks of aerobic exercise** and claim them as your own. Aerobic exercise stimulates metabolism, suppresses an overeager appetite, improves self-image, and aids the complexion with increased circulation. It also encourages the production of endorphins, natural chemical compounds within the body that make you feel relaxed, at ease, and convinced that all's right with your world.

480. ■ **The more muscle mass your body has, the more fat you'll burn,** even when you're resting. Resistance exercise (weight training) can help provide this, along with improving the shape and tone of your muscles. Weight training at least two times a week on nonconsecutive days should bring about pleasing results. "Spot reducing," however, is a myth that has taken too long to die. Aerobic exercise burns fat wherever it's deposited in the body. Heredity determines which areas give up their fat stores most readily.

481. ■ **Become an active person in your life as a whole.** In addition to your regular aerobic and resistance exercise, get incidental exercise by parking your car at the far end of the lot, opting for stairs over elevators, and getting your own glass of water from the kitchen instead of relying on a well-trained family member. If you can, develop a mobile lifestyle. Can you walk to the post office, dry cleaners, or bank from your home or office instead of driving? Do you? Who mows the lawn, cleans the house, walks the dog? They're not the most glamorous jobs on earth, but a body can benefit from them nonetheless.

And check into active recreation. If you've always wanted to try cross-country skiing, rock climbing, or something tamer like tennis, waiting for "someday" won't accomplish much. Even if the pursuit you choose isn't certifiably aerobic, it will go far toward convincing your body and mind that they're part of an active human being. They'll respond in kind.

SLIM FOR KEEPS

482. ■ **To give excess body fat short shrift, tone up your metabolism** instead of going on a diet. Do this with aerobic exercise and replacing fat calories with satisfying carbohydrate calories. This replacement means you can eat twice as much for the same amount of calories, and you'll avoid the calories from excess fat that are readily converted into body fat. (The body prefers to use carbo calories for energy rather than go to the trouble of converting them into fat to store.)

■ BONUS TIP: *Give yourself the psychological advantage of a positively worded message instead of a negatively worded one. You don't have to think of yourself as eating less fat so much as eating more complex carbohydrates.*

483. ▪ **Alcohol inhibits the body's capacity to burn fat.** Therefore, drink alcohol moderately if at all.

484. ▪ **Refined sugar is less adept at satisfying an appetite** than complex carbos are. Besides, sugar is usually found teamed with fat. Satisfy your sweet tooth with fruits and whole-grain desserts and keep hunger at bay with natural, low-fat meals and snacks.

485. ▪ **Eat enough.** Internist John McDougall, author of *The McDougall Program* and other books, says that one of the causes of obesity is not eating enough starch.

486. ▪ **Get plenty of rest and sleep.** Fatigue can easily be misinterpreted as a potato chip deficiency.

487. ▪ **If you're a professional dieter, make a career change.** Depriving yourself of food *makes you fatter.* It does this in two ways. First, the natural response to deprivation—physically and psychologically—is to overeat as soon as the opportunity presents itself. Second, the body interprets calorie restriction as famine and once the period of restraint is over, it wisely works to conserve as many calories as possible in the form of body fat.

And most diets aren't carried to completion anyway. One slip implies failure and that's the end of the diet. Eating low-fat, high-complex carbohydrate foods is a habit shift that's for life. If you eat other foods sometimes and have an occasional day when you consume more fat than usual, you haven't "broken your diet" because you're not on one.

▪ BONUS TIP: *Educate yourself thoroughly on this new approach to food and weight to reprogram a diet mentality into a nondiet one. I recommend* Eat More, Weigh Less, *by Dean Ornish, M.D., and* A Physician's Slimming Guide, *by Neal Barnard, M.D.*

488. Keeping a food diary is also helpful for some people.

That way you can see if you're having french fries once in a blue moon or every time there is a moon. One person I know got into the swing of low-fat eating by keeping her basic food diary in black ink and using red for rich foods. Any day her diary looked like a field of poppies, there was visual evidence she'd gone overboard.

489. ■ **Accept your body the way it is today** and trust that your dedication to regular exercise and eating a low-fat, high-complex carbohydrate diet is getting you in better shape every day. The process takes time. This is not some crash diet that will make you thin in two weeks and fat again two weeks later. Exercise and low-fat eating will instead create within your body an environment that is inhospitable to the storage of extra fat.

490. ■ **If you routinely eat foods you wish you didn't** and no amount of motivation has been able to change that, or if you go on eating binges, or frequently use food for emotional solace, you may need help that goes beyond dietary knowledge. My previous book, *The Love-Powered Diet,* explores these issues. I also recommend the recovery program and peer support of a group such as Overeaters Anonymous.

THE REST OF THE WORLD

491. ■ **Spend time with friends who have cut the fat, too.** Life can be lonely when you're the only person you know who doesn't eat double hamburgers or who questions the amount of cheese on a pizza. More and more people in every age group, however, are cutting fat for one reason or another. If you don't find enough of them within your circle of friends, affiliate with a group. Sometimes health clubs, hospitals, and community health organizations sponsor seminars and social events for people interested in feeling better and becoming more fit.

You can also connect with a local vegetarian organization. You don't have to be a full-time vegetarian to partake of these groups' scrumptious dinners or participate in their informative classes and workshops. And don't let the old stereotype of a vegetarian keep you away. The people you'll meet at these events are average Americans—business and professional people, students, parents. You will not be greeted at the door with "Hey, man, it's groovy you're here."

492. ■ **Persevere, even if your family resists your dietary change.** If your partner is open to learning about the benefits of low-fat dining, terrific. You can cook together and take walks together—that would improve any relationship! (In the Ornish program, cooking classes and support group sessions are not just for patients but for spouses as well.) Sometimes, however, we have to take care of ourselves even when those close to us find that threatening.

493. ■ **Influence others with your own success.** There are few creatures more insufferable than dietary evangelists. (I once heard a woman shriek to her husband as he made his selection in a cafeteria line: "Don't you know how much fat is in that?" If he hadn't known before, he certainly knew then, and so did about fifty other people.) "Live and let live" has only become a cliché because of the wisdom in it. Not everyone wants to do what we do. The surest way we can encourage others is to keep quiet, improve our health, and become fitter than we've been in years. "Example," my grandmother always said, "is not the best teacher: it's the only teacher." (Emerson probably said that first. My grandmother was always saying something profound that turned out to be from Emerson.)

494. ■ **Help your children develop healthful "memory**

foods." We all have foods that we associate with positive early experiences and we like those foods all our lives. Mine are plain sponge cake and soft-serve ice cream—vanilla. But the stuff of those good memories for our children can be air-popped corn, the summer's first strawberries, watermelon picnics, oatmeal in the morning, brown bread in the oven, and a garden of their own.

495. ■ **When you entertain, stick with recognizable foods** that people are used to having without much fat: pasta, rice dishes, vegetable stir-fries, black beans and corn bread, thick soup with a hot loaf of whole wheat or rye. You may wish to provide butter, oil-based salad dressing, and cream for coffee if you think your guests will really want them. But with so many people conscious of fat nowadays, they'll probably appreciate a low-fat meal at your house, whether they consistently treat themselves this well or not. (For inspiration on low-fat socializing, you may wish to refer to *Entertaining Light: Healthy Company Menus with Great Style* by Martha Rose Shulman.)

HEALTHY ATTITUDES, HEALTHY LIFE

496. ■ **Think of yourself as a fit, healthy person** who is getting the fat off your body and out of your life. Your body instinctively follows the pattern set by your mind.

497. ■ **Upgrade your diet overall** as well as cutting its fat. Eat natural foods that are high in fiber, complex carbohydrates, minerals, and vitamins. Let fat-reduced snack foods and sweets be fun adjuncts to your diet, not its basis. In addition:

498. ■ **Get plenty of raw foods—fresh fruit and salads—** and steam or stir-fry modestly so vegetables keep their crunch and their vitamins.

499. ■ **Obtain the highest-quality food you can**—whole foods instead of fragmented ones, organically grown when possible, minimally processed, and at their peak of freshness.

500. ■ **Eat identifiable food.** If the label reads like a chemistry text, the food in the package is probably not something the cells of your body would put on their shopping list.

■ BONUS TIP: *Give yourself time to yourself to be quiet and reflect. Having a period of stillness each day can be of value in mitigating the stress that inevitably accompanies changing habits. In addition, quieting the mind in this way has been shown to have its own positive effects physiologically (helping to normalize blood pressure, for example). In this way, your quiet time can work hand in hand with your new manner of eating to bring about desired physical results. (For help in learning to still your mind and body, read a book such as* The Relaxation Response *by Herbert Benson, M.D., or* Choose to Live Peacefully, *by Susan Smith Jones, Ph.D.)*

501. ■ **Treat yourself often,** both with the low-fat foods you really enjoy and with nonedible comforts such as hot baths, first-run movies, relaxing massages, and frequent reminders of what a great job you're doing.

AFTERWORD

The other day I was in the salad-dressing aisle at the supermarket. The veterinarian had told me that putting a little full-fat blue cheese dressing on my cat's food might make her more enthusiastic about her prescription geriatric kibble. It took me three read-throughs of the dressing labels to find a bottle of blue cheese that wasn't "light," "low fat," "fat reduced," or in some other way altered to be less appealing to elderly cats and more appropriate for human beings trying to take care of themselves.

Things are changing. Chefs are creating more low-fat dishes. Doctors and dietitians are offering more low-fat counsel. Insurance companies are beginning to recognize that medical programs promoting dietary and lifestyle modifications are effective both clinically and fiscally. Many observers believe that government recommendations may soon be revised to more closely comply with the lower fat intakes suggested as ideal by many careful studies.

This means that life is getting a lot less complicated for anyone who wants to get the fat out! Nutritious, low-fat foods are available in abundance and dining healthfully in restaurants has never been easier. It wasn't long ago that someone attempting to eat well was the odd person out. Now virtually all the people I know are trying in some way to minimize their dietary fat. Somehow when I wasn't looking, eating smart became the thing to do.

That's good news for all of us who want to provide the best foods we can for the only bodies we've got. It may be less than wonderful news for me as an author because so many innovative low-fat and nonfat products are coming out that I'd have to write an addendum a day to keep up with them all. The basic tips presented here, however, will serve you favorably for years to come.

Remember those New Four Food Groups: whole grains, vegetables, legumes, and fruits. Think of them as your core nourishers. Choose the best foods you can afford, those that feed your body, your senses, and your spirit with their color, scent, and flavor. Taste every mouthful and savor every bite. Throughout history, dining has been seen as a social rite, a celebration, even a religious ritual. Eating a bagel and jam on the train may not qualify for that list, but it can't hurt to think of it as an amazing thing, this food that buys another day on earth.

Treat yourself as well as you know how, at mealtime and the rest of the day. Enjoy the fact that you have energy to spare, a body it feels good to live in, and a doctor who may be rich, but not from your money. It's a little thing, changing the food you eat. But in your life it can make an enormous difference.

APPENDIX

H ere are seven days of sample menus—and "sample" is the most important word in the sentence. These fantasy menus are to provide you with ideas, not what you'll actually eat next Tuesday. Real-life eating is almost never like menus in books. It involves polishing off leftovers, accepting last-minute dinner invitations, burning the stew and ending up with sandwiches. Low-fat eating can accommodate all such eventualities.

When you plan your own menus, allow yourself to be influenced by the season of the year and the produce that is freshest and most prolific. And remember the curious paradox of healthful eating: *simplicity* and *variety*. Your meals never have to be complicated (who has the time?), but over the day, the week, and the month you can eat a wide variety of foods, both to meet your nutrient needs and to keep things interesting.

■ MONDAY ■

Breakfast—Sliced bananas and strawberries with strawberry nonfat or soy yogurt

Lunch—Black bean soup
Sourdough bread
Crudités: broccoli, cauliflower, green pepper, celery with Garbanzo "Nut Butter" (tip 312)

Dinner—Vegetable stew: potatoes, carrots, onions, parsnips
Tossed green salad with seasoned rice vinegar
Fat-free corn bread (tip 74) with fruit jam
Baked apples

Snack—Frozen fruit-juice "pop" (tip 337)

■ TUESDAY ■

Breakfast—Oil-free granola (tip 110) with nonfat milk or low-fat soy milk
Seasonal fresh fruit

Lunch—Vegetarian chili (or chili con carne with half the meat and twice the beans)
Oil-free corn chips (tip 437)
Raw vegetables—peppers, celery, tomatoes—with salsa

Dinner—Spinach salad with Dijon and lemon dressing (tip 147)
Vegetable stir-fry (tip 299)
Brown rice (tip 224)
Tofu cheesecake (tip 381)

Snack—Toasted chick-peas (tip 335)

■ WEDNESDAY ■

Breakfast—Smoothie: Grape or apple juice, banana, frozen strawberries, and nonfat milk powder or soy milk powder

Lunch—Cheeseless, baked crust pizza topped with mushrooms, onion, garlic, broccoli
No-oil minestrone soup

Dinner—Tossed salad of leafy greens with garbanzos and Choose to Be Fat-Free Salad Dressing (tip 161)
Baked sweet potatoes with plain nonfat or soy yogurt
Steamed collards or kale with garlic (tip 297)
Lemon or raspberry sorbet

Snack—Air-popped corn with tamari soy sauce, garlic powder, chili powder

■ THURSDAY ■

Breakfast—Citrus slices—orange, grapefruit, or tangerine
    Whole wheat–blueberry English muffins
    All-fruit jam

Lunch—Pasta salad with garden vegetables
    Sprouted wheat bread baked garlic spread (tip 243)
    Fresh or bottled mixed vegetable juice

Dinner—Mexican buffet: Oil-free refried beans (tip 272)
    Green pea guacamole (tip 166)
    Tomatoes, scallions, peppers, lettuce
    Warmed corn tortillas (tip 274)
    Tropical fruit salad: mango, papaya, pineapple

Snack—Fruit-flavored nonfat or soy yogurt

■ FRIDAY ■

Breakfast—Oatmeal or other hot whole-grain cereal with chopped
    apples and dates
    Fresh fruit or vegetable juice

Lunch—Salad sandwiches in whole wheat pita pockets
    Fat-free potato chips (tip 328)
    Carrot sticks
    Fat-free pudding (tip 379 or 380)

Dinner—Salad of baby greens with Lime Yogurt Vinaigrette
    (tip 163)
    Evolutionary Quiche (tofu) with brown rice crust (tip 225) or
    baked haddock with lemon
    Steamed broccoli
    Poached Bananas (tip 352) with Brandied Dried Fruits
    (tip 355)

Snack—Chunky Apple Spice Muffin (tip 80)

■ SATURDAY ■

Breakfast—Basic Pancakes (tip 97) with sliced fresh fruit and real
   maple syrup

Lunch—Vegetable soup
   Fat-free crackers
   Broccoli and cauliflower florets with tofu dip (tip 171)
   Carrot Cake (tip 388)

Dinner—Angel hair pasta with oil-free fresh tomato sauce (tip 211)
   Fat-free garlic bread (tip 243)
   Green salad with fennel, radicchio, and Italian Marinade
   (tip 155)
   Pears and grapes

Snack—Rice cakes with fruit jam

■ SUNDAY ■

Breakfast—No-cholesterol French toast with applesauce
   (tip 91 or 92)
   Mixed vegetable juice

Lunch—Large salad of assorted fruits with Mock Whipped Cream
   (tip 392)
   Lettuce leaves and celery stalks
   Oil-free gingerbread (tip 386)

Dinner—Boston baked beans
   Fresh whole-grain bread
   Red and white cabbage slaw with Dressing for Healthy
   Coleslaw (tip 154)
   Apple Crisp (tip 377)

Snack—Warm nonfat or soy milk with cocoa or carob

■ ■ ■

BIBLIOGRAPHY

▪ BOOKS ▪

New concepts need continual reinforcement to become your own. The books listed below can provide some of that, as well as a more detailed look at some of the topics we've touched on. Had there been room in Get the Fat Out *for one more tip, it would have been: Keep reading!*

Adler, Bill, and Heather Harvey. *The Anti-Cancer, Heart Attack, Stroke Diet.* Nashville: T. Nelson, 1991.

American Heart Association. *The American Heart Association Fat & Cholesterol Counter.* New York: Times Books/Random House, 1991.

Atlas, Nava. *American Harvest: Regional Recipes for the Vegetarian Kitchen.* New Paltz, NY: Adam Enterprises, 1991.

———. *Soups for All Seasons: Bountiful Vegetarian Soups.* New Paltz, NY: Adam Enterprises, 1992.

———. *Vegetarian Celebrations: Healthy Menus for Holidays & Other Festive Occasions.* Boston: Little, Brown, 1990.

Bailey, Covert. *The New Fit or Fat.* Boston: Houghton Mifflin, 1991.

———. *The Fit or Fat Target Diet: The Easiest Plan for Your Best Diet.* Houghton Mifflin, 1984.

Barnard, Neal, M.D., with recipes by Jennifer Raymond. *Food for Life: How the New Four Food Groups Can Save Your Life.* New York: Harmony Books, 1993.

———. *A Physician's Slimming Guide: For Permanent Weight Control.* Summertown, TN: The Book Publishing Co., 1992.

———. *The Power of Your Plate: Eating Well for Better Health—17*

Experts Tell You How. Summertown, TN: The Book Publishing Co., 1990.

Beltz, Muriel. *Cooking with Natural Foods.* HCR 89, Box 167, Hermosa, SD: Black Hills Health & Education Center, 1981.

Benson, Herbert, M.D., and Miriam Z. Klipper. *The Relaxation Response.* New York: Avon Books, 1976.

Braunstein, Mark M. *The Sprout Garden: The Indoor Grower's Guide to Gourmet Sprouts.* Summertown, TN: The Book Publishing Co., 1993.

Carroll, Mary, and Hal Straus. *The No-Cholesterol (No Kidding!) Cookbook: The Medically Proven Kitchen Cure for High Cholesterol.* Emmaus, PA: Rodale Press, 1991.

Center for Conservative Therapy. *Simply Good Recipes & More.* Mount Vernon, WA: Get Well/Stay Well, America, 1989.

Diamond, Marilyn. *The American Vegetarian Cookbook from the Fit for Life Kitchen.* New York: Warner Books, 1990.

Dinshah, Freya. *The Vegan Kitchen.* 501 Old Harding Highway, Malaga, NJ: American Vegan Society, 1992.

Dujovne, Carlos A., M.D., Jolene Held, R.D., Gloria Peterson, William S. Harris, Ph.D., and Leslie Votaw, M.S., R.D., coordinating editor. *A Change of Heart: Steps to Healthy Eating,* 2nd. ed. 1900 W. 47 Place, Suite 110, Westwood, KS: Professional Nutrition Systems, 1993.

Havala, Suzanne, M.S., R.D., and Mary Clifford, R.D. *Simple, Lowfat, & Vegetarian: Unbelievably Easy Ways to Reduce the Fat in Your Meals.* P.O. Box 1463, Baltimore, MD: The Vegetarian Resource Group, 1994.

Hurd, Rosalie, and Frank Hurd, D.C., M.D. *Ten Talents.* Box 86-A, Route 1, Chisholm, MN: Dr. and Mrs. Frank Hurd, 1985.

Jones, Susan Smith, Ph.D. *Choose to Be Healthy.* Berkeley, CA: Celestial Arts, 1987.

———. *Choose to Live Peacefully.* Berkeley, CA: Celestial Arts, 1991.

———. *Choose to Live Each Day Fully.* Berkeley, CA: Celestial Arts, 1994.

Kradjian, Robert M., M.D. *Save Yourself from Breast Cancer.* New York: Berkley Publishing, 1994.

Kurzweil, Raymond. *The 10% Solution for a Healthy Life.* New York: Crown Publishers, Inc., 1993.

Leggatt, Jenny. *Cooking with Flowers.* New York: Ballantine, 1988.

Mateljan, George. *Cooking Without Fat.* Irwindale, CA: Health Valley Foods, 1992.

McDougall, John A., M.D. *The McDougall Program: Twelve Days to Dynamic Health.* New York: NAL-Dutton, 1991.

———. *McDougall's Medicine: A Challenging Second Opinion.* Hampton, NJ: New Win, 1986.

McDougall, John A., M.D., and Mary A. McDougall. *The McDougall Plan: For Super Health and Life-Long Weight Loss.* Hampton, NJ: New Win, 1985.

McDougall, Mary A. *The McDougall Plan Recipes, Vol. I.* Hampton, NJ: New Win, 1985.

———. *The McDougall Plan Recipes, Vol. II.* Hampton, NJ: New Win, 1986.

Messina, Virginia, M.P.H., R.D., and Kate Schumann. *The No-Cholesterol Vegetarian Barbecue Cookbook.* New York: St. Martin's Press, 1994.

Moran, Victoria. *The Love-Powered Diet: A Revolutionary Approach to Healthy Eating and Recovery from Food Addiction.* San Rafael, CA: New World Library, 1992.

Ornish, Dean, M.D. *Dr. Dean Ornish's Program for Reversing Heart Disease: The Only System Scientifically Proven to Reverse Heart Disease Without Drugs or Surgery.* New York: Random House, 1990.

———. *Eat More, Weigh Less: Dr. Dean Ornish's Life Choice Program for Losing Weight Safely While Eating Abundantly.* New York: HarperCollins, 1993.

Pickarski, Ron, O.F.M. *Friendly Foods: Gourmet Vegetarian Cuisine.* Berkeley, CA: Ten Speed Press, 1991.

Pritikin, Nathan, and Patrick M. McGrady, Jr. *The Pritikin Program for Diet & Exercise.* New York: Bantam Books, 1980.

Pritikin, Robert. *The New Pritikin Program: The Easy and Delicious Way to Shed Fat, Lower Your Cholesterol, & Stay Fit.* New York: Simon & Schuster, 1990.

Raymond, Jennifer. *The Peaceful Palate: Fine Vegetarian Cuisine.* 284 Margarita Ave., Palo Alto, CA: Jennifer Raymond, 1992.

Robbins, John, with recipes by Jia Patton and friends. *May All Be Fed: Diet for a New World.* New York: William Morrow, 1992.

Rose, Norman. *Just No Fat: No Fat Cooking with Over 400 Recipes of Regular Food for Regular People from Chili Dogs to Cheesecake.* P.O. Box 8009, Shawnee Mission, KS: Diets End, 1992.

————. *No Fat Please: Feast Without Fat & Lose Weight.* P.O. Box 8009, Shawnee Mission, KS: Diets End, 1991.

Saltzman, Joanne. *Amazing Grains: Creating Vegetarian Main Dishes with Whole Grains.* Tiburon, CA: H. J. Kramer, Inc., 1990.

————. *Romancing the Bean: Essentials for Creating Vegetarian Bean Dishes.* Tiburon, CA: H. J. Kramer, 1993.

Sass, Lorna. *Cooking Under Pressure.* New York: William Morrow & Co., 1989.

————. *Recipes from an Ecological Kitchen.* New York: William Morrow & Co., 1992.

Shulman, Martha Rose. *Entertaining Light: Healthy Company Menus with Great Style.* New York: Bantam Books, 1991.

Shurtleff, William, and Akiko Aoyagi. *The Book of Tempeh: The Perfect Protein—Cholesterol Free.* New York: HarperCollins, 1985.

Stepaniak, Joanne, and Kathy Hecker. *Ecological Cooking: Recipes to Save the Planet.* Summertown, TN: The Book Publishing Co., 1992.

Stern, Ellen, and Jonathan Michaels. *The Good Heart Diet Cookbook: No Meat, No Oil, No Egg, No Butter, No Sugar, Low Salt.* New York: Ticknor & Fields, 1982.

Stillman, Joan. *Fast and Low: Easy Recipes for Low-Fat Cuisine.* Boston: Little, Brown & Co., 1985.

Wagner, Lindsay, and Ariane Spade. *The High Road to Health: A Vegetarian Cookbook.* New York: Prentice Hall Press, 1990.

Warshaw, Hope S., M.M.Sc., R.D. *The Healthy Eater's Guide to Family & Chain Restaurants: What to Eat in Over 100 Chains Across America.* Minneapolis: Chronimed Publications, 1993.

Wasserman, Debra. *The Lowfat Jewish Vegetarian Cookbook: Healthy Traditions from Around the World.* P.O. Box 1463, Baltimore, MD: The Vegetarian Resource Group, 1994.

————, with nutrition section by Reed Mangels, Ph.D., R.D. *Simply Vegan: Quick Vegetarian Recipes.* P.O. Box 1463, Baltimore, MD: The Vegetarian Resource Group, 1991.

Whitaker, Julian, M.D. *Reversing Health Risks: How to Get Out of the High-Risk Category for Cancer, Heart Disease, & Other Health Problems.* New York: G. P. Putnam's Sons, 1988.

Williams, Jacqueline, and Goldie Silverman. *No Salt, No Sugar, No Fat Cookbook: An Easy, Delicious Approach to Good Health.* San Leandro, CA: Nitty Gritty Cookbooks/Bristol Publishing Enterprises, 1993.

▪ PERIODICALS ▪

I must admit to a fondness for books. After all, I write them. Nevertheless, when you're newly inspired from reading a book, you can feel like the only person on earth who's so informed. Periodicals that show up in your mailbox can affirm your intentions every month or two. A great many publications run frequent articles on low-fat dining. The list below concentrates on publications that deal almost exclusively with healthy eating. This list below is by no means exhaustive. Start with these leads, and go beyond them. These publications are available at newsstands and by subscription unless otherwise indicated.

Ahimsa (membership journal of The American Vegan Society), 501 Old Harding Highway, Malaga, NJ 08328

Cooking Light: The Magazine of Food & Fitness, 2100 Lakeshore Drive, Birmingham, AL 35209

Delicious! (complimentary to natural foods store shoppers; also available by subscription), 1301 Spruce Street, Boulder, CO 80302

Eating Well: The Magazine of Food & Health, Ferry Road, Charlotte, VT 05445

Health Science (membership journal of The American Natural Hygiene Society), P.O. Box 30630, Tampa, FL 33630

Good Medicine (membership journal of Physicians Committee for Responsible Medicine), 5100 Wisconsin Avenue, #404, Washington, DC 20016

Nutrition Action (a publication of Center for Science in the Public Interest), P.O. Box 96611, Washington, DC 20090-6611

Vegetarian Gourmet, 2 Public Avenue, Montrose, PA 18801-1220
Vegetarian Journal (membership journal of The Vegetarian Resource Group, also at newsstands), P.O. Box 1463, Baltimore, MD 21203
Vegetarian Times, 1140 Lake Street, Suite 500, Oak Park, IL 60301
Vegetarian Voice (membership journal of The North American Vegetarian Society), P.O. Box 52, Dolgeville, NY 13329
Veggie Life, 1041 Shary Circle, Concord, CA 94518
Weight Watchers Magazine, 360 Lexington Avenue, NY 10017-6547

PERMISSIONS

The author gratefully acknowledges permission to use recipes from:

The American Vegetarian Cookbook from the Fit for Life Kitchen, by
Marilyn Diamond. Copyright © 1990 by Harvey and Marilyn
Diamond's Fit for Life, Inc. Reprinted by permission from
Warner Books/New York.

Cooking with Natural Foods, by Muriel Beltz, 4th ed., Sept. 1981,
Library of Congress Card #86-063071, ISBN 0-912145-15-3.
Reprinted by permission of Muriel Beltz.

Cooking Without Fat, by George Mateljan. Copyright © 1992 by
Health Valley Foods. Reprinted by permission from Health Valley Foods, Irwindale, California.

Dr. Dean Ornish's Program for Reversing Heart Disease, by Dean
Ornish, M.D. Copyright © 1990 by Dean Ornish, M.D.
Reprinted by permission of Random House, Inc.

Ecological Cooking: Recipes to Save the Planet, by Joanne Stepaniak and
Kathy Hecker. Copyright © 1991 by Joanne Stepaniak and
Kathy Hecker. Reprinted by permission of The Book Publish-
ing Co., Summertown, Tennessee.

Fast and Low: Easy Recipes for Low-Fat Cusine, by Joan Stillman.
Copyright © 1985 by Joan Stillman. By permission of Little,
Brown and Company, Boston.

Food for Life: How the New Four Food Groups Can Save Your Life, by
Neal Barnard, M.D., with recipes by Jennifer Raymond. Copy-
right © 1993 by Neal Barnard, M.D., Chapter 8 copyright © by
Jennifer Raymond. Reprinted by permission of Harmony Books,
New York.

The Good Heart Diet Cookbook, by Ellen Stern and Jonathan MIchaels. Copyright © 1982 by Ellen Stern and Jonathan Michaels. Reprinted by permission of Ticknor & Fields/Houghton Mifflin Co., New York. All rights reserved.

Health Science (membership journal of the American Natural Hygiene Society), recipe by Sue Douglas. Reprinted by permission of the American Natural Hygiene Society, Tampa, Florida.

The High Road to Health, by Lindsay Wagner and Ariane Spade. Copyright © 1990 by Lindsay Wagner and Ariane Spade. Used by permission of the publisher, Prentice Hall Press/a Division of Simon & Schuster, New York.

Just No Fat, by Norman Rose. Copyright © 1992 by Norman Rose. ISBN 0-9631847-1-7. Reprinted by permission of Norman Rose.

The McDougall Health-Supporting Cookbook, Vol. 1, by Mary A. McDougall. Copyright © 1985 by Mary A. McDougall. Reprinted by permission of Mary A. McDougall.

The McDougall Plan, by John McDougall, M.D., and Mary A. McDougall. Copyright © 1983 by John A. McDougall, MD., and Mary A. McDougall. Reprinted by permission of Mary A. McDougall.

No Salt, No Sugar, No Fat Cookbook, by Jacqueline B. Williams with Goldie Silverman. Copyright © 1993, 1981 by Bristol Publishing Enterprises, Inc. Reprinted with permission of Bristol Publishing Enterprises, Inc., San Leandro, California.

The Peaceful Palate, by Jennifer Raymond. Copyright © 1992 by Jennifer Raymond. Reprinted by permission of Jennifer Raymond.

The Pritikin Program for Diet & Exercise, by Nathan Pritikin and Patrick McGrady. Copyright © 1979 by Nathan Pritikin and Patrick McGrady. Reprinted by permission of Alan Goldhamer, D.C.

Simply Vegan, by Debra Wasserman. Copyright © 1991 by Debra Wasserman. Reprinted by permission of Debra Wasserman, The Vegetarian Resource Group, Baltimore.

Ten Talents, by Rosalie Hurd and Frank Hurd, D.C., M.D. Copyright © 1968 and 1985 by Frank J. Hurd and Rosalie Hurd. Reprinted by permission of Rosalie Hurd.

INDEX

Appetizers, 116–118
Apple crisp, 129
Apple spice muffins, 38–39
Applesauce, horseradish, 97
Attitude, 166–167

Baking, 119–121, 124–127
Banana-date cookies, 134–135
Banana french bread, 42
Bananas, poached, 122–123
Barbecue sauce, 56
Barnard, Dr. Neal, 15
Bean bake, easy, 90–91
Beans, 89–91
Black bean soup, 71
Braunstein, Mark M., 54
Breads, 36–39, 42
Breakfast beverages, 49–50
Broccomole, 65
Brown gravy, simple, 81–82
Brown sugar-raisin
    cookies, 133

Cakes, 136–137
Calories, *xiii*, 9–11
Calories, percentage of from fat,
    3–4
Campbell, T. Colin, 11, 14–15
Carroll, Mary, 60, 79
Carrot cake, 136–137
Castelli, Dr. William, 9
Cereals, 46–48
Cherries, thickened, 40–41
China study, 10–11
Chocolate chip cookies,
    133–134
Chocolate pudding, 130–131
Chocolate sauce, 140
Cholesterol, *xiii*, 5–6, 9–10
Cookies, 133–135
Cooking techniques, 21–25
Cookware, 25–27
Corn, creamed, 41
Corn bread, 37
Corny butter, 39

Diamond, Marilyn, 77
Diet, getting started, 155–159
Dips, 63–66
Douglas, Sue, 65

Eating on the run, 150–153
Eating out, 141–145
Egg substitutes, 42–43
Exercise, 160–162

Farmington Heart Study, 9–11
Fiesta foods, 97–98
Fillers, 109–111
Fish, *xii*
Forsberg, Michael, 76
Frozen treats, 137–140
Fruit fondue, carob, 123
Fruits, 121–124
Fruits, brandied dried, 124

Garbanzo flour gravy, 82–83
Garbanzo "nut" butter, 111
Gingerbread, 135–136
Grains, 86–88
Granola, 47–48
Gravy, 81–83
Green pea "guacamole," 64

HDLs/LDLs, 6, 10
Herb sauce, oil-free, 77–78
High-fat diets and health,
    1–3
Hors d'oeuvres, 116–118
Hurd, Rosalie
    and Dr. Frank, 68

Influence, 164–166
International restaurants,
    147–150
Italian marinade, 60

Jensen, Bernard, 68
Jolliffe, Dr. Norman, *xii*
Jones, Susan Smith, 61

LDLs/HDLs, 6, 10
Lime yogurt vinaigrette, 62–63

McGrady, Patrick, Jr., 77
Maintaining, 162–164
Marshall, Gladys, 63
Mary's Canadian Campout
    Dressing, 58
Mateljan, George, 60
Meats, 98–103
Menu savvy, 145–147
Menus, a week of sample,
    170–173
Miller, Kathy, 55
Moderation, 32–34
Monounsaturated fats, 6–8

New Four Food Groups, 12–14

Onion soup, 72
Ornish, Dr. Dean, 9, 12,
    13, 15, 64

Pancakes, 44–45
Pasta, 78–81, 91–92

Pesto, low-fat, 79
Pie, Freya's no-crust blueberry, 127–128
Pierce, Sonnet, 80
Pies, 127–129
Polyunsaturated fats, 6
Potato salad, 54
Potatoes, 93–97
Potatoes, Pat's home fries, 94
Potatoes, scalloped, 95
Pritikin program, 13, 77
Puddings, 130–32
Pumpkin, stuffed, 103–104

Quiche, evolutionary, 87

Rice, 86–89

Salad dressing, 57–62
Salad dressing, fat-free, 62
Salads, 52–56
Saltzman, Joanne, 79
Sandwiches, 107, 109–111
Sanell, Richard, 51–52
Saturated fats, 5–6
Sauces, 75–78, 97
Shopping, 27–28
Side dishes, 84–86
Silverman, Goldie, 76

Snacks, 113–116
Soups, 67, 70–75
Spice, 29–32
Spice paste, 31
Spice shelf veggie dip, 63–66
Spreads, 39–42, 109–111
Stillman, Joan, 57
Stock, 68–70

Thailandish peanut sauce, 80
Tofu, *xiii*, 43
Tofu "cheesecake," 131–132
Tofu dip, 66
Toppings, 137–140
Trader, Tim, 54
Twain, Mark, 15

USDA Food Guide Pyramid, 11–12

Vegetable broth, 68–69
Vegetable neat loaf, 99–100
Vegetables, 104–106
Veggie-cheez sauce, 75–76

Waffles, 45–46
Walnuts, mock black, 127
Whipped cream, mock, 138
White sauce, 76
Williams, Jacqueline B., 76

ABOUT THE AUTHOR

VICTORIA MORAN has been writing about healthy eating for more than twenty years. Her articles have appeared in publications including *American Health, EastWest (Natural Health), Vegetarian Times,* and *Weight Watchers* magazine. She is also the author of *The Love-Powered Diet: A Revolutionary Approach to Healthy Eating and Recovery from Food Addiction.*

For more information on other materials from the author and her lectures and workshops in your area, send a stamped, self-addressed envelope to PeaceMeal, P.O. Box 20301, Country Club Plaza Station, Kansas City, MO 64112.